I BELIEVE, DESPITE EVERYTHING

I BELIEVE, DESPITE EVERYTHING

Reflections of an Ecumenist

J.-M. R. Tillard, O.P.

Translated by
William G. Rusch

Foreword by
Mary Tanner

LITURGICAL PRESS
Collegeville, Minnesota

www.litpress.org

A title of the Unitas Books series published by the Liturgical Press

Cover design by McCormick Creative, with Katty Montenegro Sacoto. Photo courtesy of Peter Williams / WCC.

First published in Italian as *Credo nonostante . . .* by Centro editoriale dehoniano

© 2000 Centro editoriale dehoniano, via Nosadella, 6 – 40123 Bologna

1   2   3   4   5   6   7   8

Library of Congress Cataloging-in-Publication Data

Tillard, J.-M. R. (Jean-Marie Roger), 1927–
    [Credo nonostante—. English]
    I believe, despite everything : reflections of an ecumenist / J.-M. R. Tillard ; translated by William G. Rusch.
       p. cm.
    ISBN 0-8146-2492-8 (alk. paper)
    1. Church. 2. Church—Unity.   I. Title.

BX1746.T52513 2003
230'.2—dc21
                                                          2003047610

Unitas Books

On the eve of his crucifixion, Jesus prayed that his followers "All may be one" (John 17:21). Christians believe that this promise is fulfilled in the Church. The Church is Christ's Body and his Body cannot be divided. And yet, the Churches today live in contradiction to that promise. Churches which recognize in another Christian community an embodiment of the one Church of Jesus Christ still too often find that they cannot live in true communion with them. This contradiction between the Church's unity and its division has driven the ecumenical movement over the last century.

The pursuit of unity will require more than a few mutual adjustments among the Churches. Ecumenism must involve true conversion, a conversion both of hearts and minds, of the will and the intellect. We all must learn to think in new ways about the teachings and practices of the Church. Division has become deeply embedded in the everyday life and thought of the Churches. Thinking beyond division will require a new outlook.

Unitas Books seeks to serve the rethinking that is a necessary part of the ecumenical movement. Some books in the series will directly address important topics of ecumenical discussion; others will chart and analyze the ecumenical movement itself. All will be concerned with the Church's unity. Their authors will be ecumenical experts from a variety of Christian traditions, but the books will be written for a wider audience of interested clergy and laypeople. We hope they will be informative for the expert and the newcomer alike.

The unity we seek will be a gift of the Holy Spirit. The Spirit works through means, however, and one of the Spirit's means is careful theological reflection and articulate communication. We hope that this series may be used by the Spirit so that the unity won by Christ may be more fully visible "so that the world may believe" (John 17:21).

Norman A. Hjelm
Michael Root
William G. Rusch

Contents

Foreword   ix
   Mary Tanner

Introduction   xv
   Timothy Radcliffe, O.P.

Interviews in Winter   1

Postscript   59
   Francesco Strazzari

Appendix   63

Foreword

Mary Tanner*

Jean Tillard left a lasting impression on those he taught, those he pastored, and all who engaged in ecumenical dialogue with him. This book is a fitting summary in his own words of his faith in God and his passion for the visible unity of the Church.

Jean Tillard was born on September 2, 1927, in Saint-Pierre-et-Miquelon, the small islands in the Gulf of St. Lawrence, off the coast of Newfoundland. He made his profession as a friar of the Order of Preachers in 1950 and was ordained priest five years later. Rumor has it that before becoming a Dominican Jean Tillard trained as an actor. His skill in holding an audience captive with an admixture of utmost seriousness, flights of imagination, and sometimes scandalous humor makes that highly plausible. He studied in Ottawa, Rome, and France, gaining doctorates in philosophy and theology, and became professor of dogmatic theology at the Dominican College in Ottawa, a post he held until his death. He taught at Salamanca, Barcelona, Brussels, and Fribourg and was a visiting lecturer in a number of theological colleges in England. He was a *peritus*, expert, at the Second Vatican Council.

No one made a greater contribution to the bilateral theological conversations between Churches that blossomed after Vatican II than Jean Tillard. He served on the international conversations between the Roman Catholic Church and the Orthodox, the Disciples of Christ, and the Anglican Communion. It is important for the sake of coherence and

* Mary Tanner served formerly as the General Secretary of the Church of England Council for Christian Unity and past Moderator of the Commission on Faith and Order of the World Council of Churches.

consistency that a few are willing to serve on more than one dialogue. Tillard gave himself unsparingly in the service of these conversations in spite of the demands of a heavy teaching schedule and the trials of travel. He always came at a subject, whether of faith or order, out of a firm foundation in the Scriptures and the Fathers. He brought new insights to controverted issues, helped to discover common ground where none seemed possible, and he was often the one to find fresh language with which to express convergence or consensus. It was often a preliminary paper of his that gave shape and direction to the final agreed statement. In documents from each of these conversations it is easy to detect his influence in striking turns of phrase and startling images. He was also able to bring the insights from these bilateral conversations to the work of the multilateral conversations of the Faith and Order Commission of the World Council of Churches. Here he made significant contributions to *Baptism, Eucharist and Ministry, Confessing the One Faith*, and the most recent document, *The Nature and Purpose of the Church*. He was one of the few in the commission who was convinced of the importance of the apostolic faith study for the future of an increasingly complex ecumenical movement. But how to revitalize the study, and how to persuade others, eluded even his creative imagination.

Throughout Tillard was a perceptive commentator on the ecumenical scene. He was thoroughly behind the calling of a Fifth World Conference on Faith and Order in 1993, thirty years after the Montreal meeting. He saw the importance of standing back and asking, "where are we, where are we going?" He was keen to test out the answer "towards *koinonia* in faith, life and witness." Indeed he, together with the Orthodox theologian John Zizioulas, was a major influence in bringing the theme of *koinonia*, communion, into the center of discussions about the nature and purpose of the Church. He was keen to affirm that on the basis of common baptism and shared faith there is an already existing degree of communion between Christians, a firm foundation on which to build.

Although Tillard never gave up his passion for the visible unity of the Church, in the last two years of his life he became not a little fearful of the complexity and "fragility" of the ecumenical scene. Anglican moves, in some provinces, to ordain women to the priesthood and the episcopate he saw as complicating the scene and he feared the tension between autonomous Orthodox Churches by a resurgence of nationalism. After the Harare Assembly of the World Council of Churches in 1998 he expressed a concern about the burgeoning African Independent

Churches. He recognized in these Churches an important example of successful inculturation, but it worried him that "each attends to its own business without bothering about the others." The sense of catholicity and interdependence, so important to the life of the Church, Tillard feared was missing. He also recognized problems in older Churches with individual Christians looking to themselves, with little sense of solidarity and community. He feared a growing fragmentation of the basis of communion in faith. And, although he was the first to agree to the importance of dialogue with those of other faiths, he was increasingly nervous that interfaith dialogue was pushing some to relativize the salvific work of Christ. He was, however, convinced that none of these dangers could be confronted by a flight into fundamentalism. He was equally convinced that no Church could answer these questions alone. "Together we must say afresh—and it can only be done together— with intelligence and from within the faith, who Jesus Christ really is, and what the Father's plan is, which was carried out through Christ."

Tillard was well read though he carried his erudition lightly. He was a prolific writer. The books that helped to establish his reputation include: *The Eucharist: Pasch of God's People*, 1964; *Devant Dieu et pour le monde. Le projet des religieux*, 1974; *Church of Churches: The Ecclesiology of Communion*, 1987; *Flesh of the Church, Flesh of Christ*, 1992; *L'Eglise locale*: *Ecclésiologie de communion et catholicité*, 1995. He is perhaps best known for his 1983 book on the ministry of the Bishop of Rome, a book which in many ways foreshadowed the papal encyclical *Ut Unum Sint*. In *The Bishop of Rome* Tillard was critical of some developments in the exercise of the papal office, yet at the same time he was faithful to a ministry of universal primacy exercised in collegiality. He was utterly convinced of the contribution that such a ministry could make to the service of the unity of the one, holy, catholic and apostolic Church.

I Believe, Despite Everything encapsulates many of Jean Tillard's thoughts over many years. It shows him wrestling with difficult issues and exudes his passion for Christian unity. Above all, the book is a statement of personal faith set within the context of dreadful problems in the world, a restless ecumenical movement, and a Roman Catholic Church that has not fully received the insights of Vatican II. Tillard is incisive in his diagnosis of the present using his personal experience of his own Church and the ecumenical movement, and his firsthand knowledge of the many parts of the world that he had visited. Tillard affirms his faith in God the Holy Trinity whose intention is "to establish a communion of bliss," a God whose mercy he is sure will lead toward the "happiness" of those created in the image of God. "I believe in the Incarnation of the Son sent not to condemn but to save." There is an almost Job-like defiance about this cry of faith in the face of suffering, the world's and his own cancer, as well as a Job-like character he finds in the silence. Through the Dominican tradition he was at home with contemplation and silence.

Most of this book is a summary of Tillard's ecclesiology, offered through a series of answers to questions put by an interrogator, a useful device in leading the reader through his thinking. He had come, through ecumenical conversations, to hold and to offer to others an ecclesiology of communion. He begins with the local church, the local eucharistic community, open to all other local churches, thus affirming their diversity, a diversity derived largely from the created order. He stresses the place and role of the episcopate, pointing out that collegiality has all too often been underrated for "primacy had banished the episcopate into obscurity." Primacy and collegiality are both necessary as was clearly seen in Vatican II. Bishops are assumed into the college, enrolled into its solidarity and unity. This Tillard sees as a guarantee "that a single and identical gospel is preached throughout the world and an identical baptism and an identical Eucharist are celebrated in spite of the diversity of places and situations." He situates the Bishop of Rome within the college, the one charged with seeing that it never strays from the apostolic witness grasped in all its depth and fullness. That the papacy needs reform he is sure, but of its necessity he has no doubts. Situated within collegiality it belongs to the fiber of the Church, it is gift. While he is critical of the Roman Curia he is equally sure that it is naïve to want to do away with it, it is necessary. In all that he says about his own Church he balances criticism and the need for repentance and reform with affection and loyalty.

Again and again as he offers his thoughts on the Church his passion for the visible unity of the Church shines through. In answering what sort of unity we are seeking he offers us no model, but rather a reflection on what kind of Christianity Churches in communion would present to the world. In spite of the divisions between the Churches and internal problems he affirms his belief in the indefectibility, the indestructibility, the permanence and continuity of the Church, justifying its mission, not because of any merit of its own but because of God's faithfulness.

The last pages of this book deserve to be read meditatively as Jean ponders "what I would become if this reference to Christ was torn from my life." "You can do with me what you want, I who understand nothing but I continue to place confidence in you, I trust in you."

This is a very personal account of Jean Tillard's faith in God and in the one, holy, catholic and apostolic Church he served with such devotion and wisdom. There is a clarity and urgency to his writing that comes from one who knows he is approaching death. Those of us who had the privilege to work closely with him for many years cannot but be grateful for this special opportunity to follow the thoughts of his last days. In these pages many of us will find encouragement to continue the search for agreement in faith that is "sufficient and required" for visible communion though we do, and will continue to, miss his presence with us. For those new to the ecumenical enterprise here is a book to inspire, a vision of what by God's grace and human obedience the Church on earth might become.

Mary Tanner
Weybridge, Surrey
Lent 2003

Introduction

Jean-Marie Tillard, distinguished heir of Father Yves Congar in his ecumenical commitment and lucid interpreter of the living tradition of the Western and Eastern Churches, published several books on the renewal of religious life and of the understanding of the Church since the Second Vatican Council. The present book is a very personal witness of a profound and restless faith. There are types of restlessness that are inventive and which create something new in society and in the Church since they are the expression of a deep confidence. "Yes, I am an uneasy Christian. I get it from my Dominican calling. We are restless." This is a restlessness which dares to call the crises of the present-day Church by their name: a crisis of inwardness, of spiritual emptiness, a crisis of ecumenism, a crisis in the acceptance of the fundamental insights of the Second Vatican Council.

But Jean-Marie Tillard is not a prophet of doom. The great "despite everything" of faith does not shrink from new challenges, for it is rooted in a personal orientation to Christ Jesus. The faith of Jean-Marie Tillard, the preacher and bold theologian, finds its expression in audacity, daring, and the proud freedom that dares to confess "the difference of the Gospel." The Church's vocation is to proclaim to humankind this Good News of hope, for "the Gospel is a message of hope and its dictates are nothing less than the merciful indication of the way to enter into the blessedness of the kingdom." For Jean-Marie Tillard, this calling defines the relation of the Church to modern societies: not condemnation, but the witness of a saved heart and of God's faithfulness to humankind.

Jean-Marie Tillard is tireless when it is a question of encouraging the renewal of the Church and of its mission in light of the unity among the different ecclesial traditions. He sees the Church as the communion of local churches in the unique and indivisible gift of the Spirit. He gives courageous guidance in speaking of the primacy of the Bishop of Rome, the role of the Curia, the relation between theologians and the Church's magisterium—themes at the center of his own theological research.

One of Jean-Marie Tillard's great concerns is that "our Christian communities know less and less of the very bases of the givens of the faith." He pleads then for a renewal of preaching and for a considerable engagement of the laity in ecclesial life.

But Jean-Marie Tillard does not get lost in vague considerations about topical questions. He steers these questions back to the depth from which true answers come: to the connection between the Eucharist and the consciousness of Christians faced with human distress and misery, to the desire to rediscover the covenant between humankind and the Gospel, to the indissoluble relation between spiritual inwardness and commitment.

This approach gives a rich flavor and a deep wisdom to the words of the book which allows us to know Jean-Marie Tillard as a great lover of the One who is the human face of the Father, Christ Jesus, who has shared with us every goodness, every suffering. "If this reference to Christ was torn out of my life, I would probably be like a ship on a starless night, having lost its compass."

It is with a deeply cordial and fraternal thanks to Jean-Marie Tillard that I entrust to readers this encouraging and committed book of a brother who, "despite everything," has never lost the joy of believing and who teaches us that the plan for the religious life aims "to liberate the depths of goodness in the person and to witness to it for God."

Rome, September 1, 2000
Brother Timothy Radcliffe, o.p.
Master of the Order of Preachers

Interviews in Winter

Let us begin with a question which is perhaps indiscreet: you sometimes quote an expression from Yossel Rakover: "I believe in the God of Israel, although he has done everything to shatter the faith which I have in him." Why?

First I should add some further detail. With many others I have long believed that the distressing prayer of Yossel Rakover was written in the Warsaw ghetto, at the time of its destruction, in the horror of suffering. I was aware of the almost sacred use that was made of it in several synagogues. I know now that it was composed in Buenos Aires in 1946 by another Jew, Zvi Kolitz, who knew neither the insurrection nor the destruction of the Warsaw ghetto. But even if this prayer is merely a literary production, and if Yossel Rakover did not exist, the prayer illustrates the true accents of a Jewish faith which, since the brutality of Hitlerism, has been asking God one question. In the presence of what appears to be YHWH's indifference, in the face of the martyrdom of his worshipers, the survivors ask: "Where were you when at Auschwitz your own people were handed over to barbarism? Why did you remain silent?" A Jewish woman, who really existed and died at Auschwitz in 1943, Etty Hillesum, gave an astonishing reply: God, she thought, had decided to do nothing alone against evil; he included his own people in his own distress; he urged them to help him.

But the cry of Auschwitz is also the cry of the psalmists ("but you, YHWH, how long?" "Why, YHWH, do you hide yourself at time of distress?" "Awake, YHWH". . .). How not to hear there Christ's cry on the cross, also for him a cry drawn from the source of the psalms? These are a question and a cry that cut across history. When therefore I quote Yossel Rakover, I am thinking about this constant question, finding in confrontation with the Shoah its maximum tragedy but going beyond

1

the context of horror. It is not therefore uniquely a matter of my own question, but of this intense question of believers, in which I place my own question. Why does God seem "to keep his distance," contrary to the attitude of Jesus, whom human distress and need never left indifferent? I am not only thinking here of the unanswered prayer. I am especially thinking of situations where, knowing what we know about God, we would expect him to intervene. . . . The ardent faith of the Church, God's apparent "indifference," such is often the agony of Christians.

One of the reasons why I revisited this text some years ago was in preparation for a meeting of young, ecumenical theologians, held in Finland under the aegis of Faith and Order. It is so unusual today to discover young persons interested in the thankless task of ecumenism that I took their questions very seriously. All the more so since I knew some of them well. I felt them to be troubled and torn. They wanted not so much reasons to be involved as some support for their faith, to believe despite everything. . . . I did not mention Yossel Rakover to them, but his question remained with me.

Why is there this concern? Are you able to explain it in more detail?

I will give you reasons for this concern, a bit at random. These reasons are not the same for Catholics and other Christians.

Let's first speak about Catholics. Being a Dominican, I cannot forget Innocent III's dream at the beginning of the thirteenth century. He saw the walls of the Church collapse. In the trajectory of the Second Vatican Council throughout almost the entire world, the Catholic Church has not directed its energies to accomplish its *aggiornamento.* Contrary to what a new generation which does not know this period spontaneously thinks, it was not entirely "a joyful enterprise," "the happiness of being freed from useless weights" *(sic).* These years were marked by sufferings, by difficult changes. It was necessary to modify liturgical life, to revise catechesis, and to learn to think in different ways. The religious orders and communities had to rewrite their constitutions. The theological faculties hurried to form a new class of professors. A new style of relation was established among bishops, presbyters, deacons, and laity. One could no longer be indifferent to Protestantism or Orthodoxy. The Roman Curia itself was urged to reform. Moreover, how to assimilate documents as new as the Declaration on Religious Liberty? For this reason, I have always refused to be harsh toward the disciples of Bishop Marcel Lefebvre: they were urged to accept a very radical change, to which a certain kind of psychology could not adapt itself. To all this was added, in some ecclesiastical settings, a climate of suspicion, a source of deep wounds. There was the accusation of protestantizing the Church, of denying the presence of the Lord in the Eucharist, and of denying the primacy of Rome. An old friend, Bishop Bugnini, who was a colleague of mine in the work on eucharistic worship, told me of the unbearable burden of these denunciations, denunciations often blessed by some high-ranking person. To be fair, I must add that the label "fundamentalist" was itself also bandied about with equal aggressiveness and lack of judgment. I received within several days a letter denouncing me as a "gravedigger" of the papacy (for having said that bishops are as necessary as the Pope) and another letter calling me a fundamentalist (for having said that the primacy of Rome is willed by God).

But this bundle of tasks, sufferings, difficulties, has been accepted with a will by the local churches, whom Paul VI urged to apply the council. They were dreaming of *un primavera*, of a springtime of the Catholic Church. Now the winter has swiftly come, before summer and the harvests. What a harsh winter! Has God forgotten the efforts of his Church? Every theology of merit put aside, was the Church not able to hope for better times? In effect, the confusion and the dysfunction of Western culture, accompanied by the explosion of the media, have created a spiritual climate that has also engulfed research on Scripture and tradition, theology, and religious practice. It has become commonplace to speak of a crisis of faith, at the very least, of the uneasiness of faith. It became the duty of Rome to be concerned about this situation. Rome has intervened with important encyclicals. But on a more concrete level, its concern has taken an unexpected turn. Rome has expressed herself by a stress on the authority of the magisterium and on the duty to submit to it. Aside from serious questions linked to the sanctity of life, little has still been done to explore the "minefields" and to seek to clear them. No one is yet ready, it seems. Consequently, many Catholics are at a loss, and they concoct "their own little Catholicism for themselves."

An obvious sign of the crisis has been the strange phenomenon of the exodus of many women and men religious and priests "changing vocation," followed by the alarming drop of admissions into the novitiate or seminary. Pastors die; no one replaces them. Perhaps for the lack of a pastor for young people, few adolescents attend Church, and few have any interest in catechesis. The rate of divorce increases; that of baptism decreases. Within families, parents no longer succeed in motivating their children in a Christian manner. Faith becomes secondary; the Church superfluous. There is a slow slide, not toward an aggressiveness against the Church—except in certain contexts—but toward indifference.

Closing its institutions, reducing its places of worship—will there be a time when the generation of still-practicing Christians disappears?—the Church loses its visibility. For many, it is reduced to the presence on television of this "pilgrim of God" who has become the Bishop of Rome, reviving the mission of Paul, and to the stirring words in favor of peace, justice, and reconciliation that he delivers. But in the landscape of our cities, eventually of our villages, the visibility of the institution is increasingly absent. Often I quote a Muslim friend, who, seeing a steeple pulled down (the congregation having sold its monastery to a secular institution), said to me: "You should weep; the minaret of our mosques writes the name of Allah above the cities, the church steeple writes that of Christ."

We cannot avoid posing a question. Are some significant groups of local churches condemned to disappear from the map of Christianity? Only memories remain of the Churches of ancient Turkey, where the theological thought of the East and West was defined and has matured. Local churches of Augustine's Africa only remain as names of destroyed episcopal sees. Some vestiges of Christendom in Upper Mesopotamia only exist as ruins serving as shelter. A French bishop, looking at the map of his diocese, confessed, "The desert is also spreading among us . . . " Granted, we do see the vigor of several Churches outside the West. Spend a Sunday in a parish in Harare, take part in a meeting of peasants near Lima, allow yourself to enter into the rhythm of the patronal celebration in Aleppo—these are experiences which show that the Church of God is indeed alive. Elsewhere, as in the Caribbean, the Church continues more unobtrusively to bring joy and hope to a suffering, poor humanity. The Church is not dead. The Church is not dying. However, even in places of great vitality, it is never totally sheltered. At Harare, the Catholic bishop of the Sudan (Paride Taban) recalled the threat that weighs on his Church, and the Christians of Nigeria have continually stressed the peril in which the tidal wave of Islam put them. The tragedy of Rwanda-Burundi, two Christian lands, unsettles the overly naive optimist. What is the reason for all this?

In other Churches also, the shadows seem to get the better of the light. The case of the Orthodox Churches without a doubt is more worrisome than that of the Catholic Church. Some young theologians participating in the meeting in Finland, and who came from behind the Iron Curtain, bore witness to this situation. Several elements come into play. Because of the famous "symphony" between the Church and the state, the Church leaders were flexible in the face of Communist power. It is this situation which, after the fall of these regimes, has provoked a deep crisis of conscience. Moreover, deprived of a well-prepared clergy, the Christian communities were then swamped by a flood of "converts" with various motives, some of whom opposed every opening and advocated an intransigent conservatism. Elsewhere quarrels with the Oriental Churches united with Rome (the Uniates), also victims of a cruel persecution, veiled the beautiful mystery of charity. We should not forget the ever-thorny questions of the autocephalous Churches and the polemics against the World Council of Churches. Why, after so much tragic suffering and so much heroic resistance, is there so little peace? With the Anglicans, the situation is obviously quite different. Nevertheless, the ordination of women and ethical problems provoke not only tensions, but divisions. There also the crisis of faith becomes troublesome. In some provinces there is no hesitation to break with the strongest principles of the Anglican tradition. This situation causes for others a "crisis of communion."

I sense here your ecumenical anxiety.

No more than the Catholic Church, the Orthodox Churches, or the Anglican Church, is ecumenism dead. On this subject, false, badly informed or tendentious things have been written. However, ecumenism is not completely well. Some texts like the Joint Declaration on the Doctrine of Justification between Catholics and Lutherans must not cause us to forget other construction sites where nothing yet has been definitively built. The impression one gets is of a ship taking on water everywhere. As soon as one hole is plugged, another is discovered. I give the example of the Lima Document on Baptism, Eucharist and Ministry (BEM). Accepted unanimously, it is criticized today in such a fashion that the Churches hesitate to use it. I also give the example of the Anglican-Catholic agreement on ministry (ARCIC). Cardinal Willebrands was able to write that the way was now clear to treat irenically problems of validity. Alas, the Anglican decision to ordain women placed a new obstacle in the way, difficult to overcome. The Catholic Church continues to ask the Orthodox Churches to accelerate their theological dialogue so that official steps toward one communion could be ratified. The Orthodox reply with the insoluble imbroglio of uniatism. The World Council of Churches itself seeks its mission, having lost the confidence of many of the Churches, including the Orthodox. Why, after so many years of efforts, so many meetings and documents, so many lives consumed by this work, is there so meager a harvest, for which changed attitudes at the grassroots do not compensate? The question of Yossel Rakover comes back to mind.

You speak of "prophets of doom" . . .

Obviously, the prophets of doom, whose voices are amply orchestrated, jump on this situation like vultures. After the Assembly of the World Council of Churches in Canberra in 1991, I remember a journalist wanted me to affirm such a view, and his disappointment at my refusal to do so. According to him the vitality of the African and non-Western Churches is the final burst of energy of a great body that had its moment and that progress will cause to disappear. It is a victim of its own success. Its teaching is so well established that it no longer is able to rely on its originality. It has played its role. From it, cultures were born, a philosophy of life and of society that have shaped a world in the act of dying. For Christianity to endure, the human person would need to change radically, return to the past. It is too late. The Church had been one of the most fertile and powerful manifestations of the force of religion. But it did not know how to transform itself. Certainly, the vigorous protest of the Gospel, which it has planted in history, will remain there as a leaven or a ferment. There will always be persons protesting against injustice, taking the part of the weak, calling on God to help. But they will be individuals coming from a secular world, not members of a Church. Often they will not even know that their attitude has its source in Christ. We must thank the Church for having engraved this message in the human conscience by its preaching, its liturgy, its action. This was, no doubt, its mission.

I mention here this opinion of a journalist because it is slowly spreading even among Christians and clergy. It is true, it forces us to ask questions of ourselves—not only of God. As in the case of the Christianity of North Africa crushed by Islam, the West has been on many levels a victim of external circumstances. The twentieth century has not been a placid century. It has known at the same time the most absolute totalitarianism and the exaltation of the autonomy of the person. Intellectual and techno-scientific research has been audacious. Christians have felt helpless. All the more so because the serious crisis opened in the last century by modernism has not been fully resolved. The faithful are stretched between two authorities: the everyday authority of the media and the authority of the Church's pulpit, and they are often driven to place their trust in the first. The language of the second, which the pastoral office does not adequately try to explain, no longer engages them. "Concepts, ways of thinking from another culture, whose importance we guess, but which do not penetrate us," explained a militant layperson, asking me to give him some keys for reading an encyclical. Many have departed from a lack of interest, from weariness. They themselves say that they no longer are witnesses of the faith. Christianity has lost this famous, contagious conviction that Catholic Action aroused. "Pasteurized" Christianity has lost its ferment, a Swiss listener commented. Parents, educators, ministers no longer knew how to speak of Christ with the authority of someone who knows what this name means and truly implies. Christ has become a name among other great names.

On another level, while everyone invokes the spirit of the Second Vatican Council, each interprets it according to either liberal or traditionalist options that drown some of the council's intentions and major decisions. The uncertainty about truth has penetrated the Churches. People no longer know what or whom to believe. Many, especially when they are confronted with personal tragedies, then make an appeal for help. "Give us back reasons for believing! You have taken them away from us . . . ."

It is thus clear that we have our faults. John Paul II has stressed them in his letter on the preparation of the Jubilee of the year 2000: "And what responsibility do they [the children of the Church] have to bear, in view of the increasing lack of religion, for not having shown the true face of God . . . ?" (*Tertio millennio adveniente* 36). Everyone has faults, our Orthodox brothers and sisters, as well as the World Council of Churches. We have foolishly contributed to proving right the journalist who explained his position to me. This is why through this crisis God is probably giving us a significant message. Ministers and laity, what have you made of the Holy Spirit? Here, especially for the West, is manifest the pneumatological deficit that the Eastern Churches denounce and that cannot be overcome merely by quotations of texts on the Spirit. In spite of our wonderful declarations, we still do not seem to know how to read the *sensus fidelium* because we still do not clearly see how to avoid a false "democratization" which denies the essential place of hierarchy and its prophetic ministry. On this point, Vatican II has not yet been fully "received." I persistently maintain that it is not a question of ill will or of what some weeks ago a superficial article described as "the fear of seeing the awakening of a laity that until now has been cleverly chloroformed." No. We do not know how to act. The regional synods have shown this tension between intention (of Rome as well as of local bishops) and fulfillment. The chapter remains open. But the Spirit seems to impel us to accomplish it quickly, in *communion* and not in conflict, without rash accusations.

But, as I have said, there are mitigating circumstances; the situation in which the Orthodox Churches were placed was tragic, the World Council is in the midst of Churches tortured by the problems of societies everywhere in the world. Then I think about the merciful faithfulness of the God of the prophets and of the psalms, as did Yossel Rakover. How would his question not rise up in our hearts? Would God have forgotten the energies expended after Vatican II, the hellish jails of the Gulags? Does he not seem to do everything to shatter the faith that we place in him, to do everything so that we should consider ourselves the last Christians and . . . to prove it to others?

You maintain the faithfulness of God. What is the basis of your conviction?

A book would be required to answer this question! I am a believer and, like Yossel Rakover, I confess one God, the Creator. I believe that the divine intention presiding over creation is the wish to establish a communion in his bliss. I also believe (with all revelation) that this Creator is a God of mercy. Therefore, despite the errors or crimes, he continues to seek to lead toward happiness the men and women whom he has created in his image and likeness. I am always astonished by the scant importance theology grants to the history of Noah. For me, these chapters are a very important part of the Old Testament. When I wish to restore my confidence in the future, I return to those chapters. I well know that the description of the Flood has its origin elsewhere, in particular in the Babylonian epic of Gilgamesh. But the terms of the covenant, concluded with what then remains of creation, are to my eyes a marvelous expression of the design of God's faithfulness: he wishes neither to curse, nor to exterminate, nor to destroy. This is why I am disturbed that he allows cursing, exterminating, destroying. The astonishment of Yossel Rakover is also mine.

However, as a Christian, I believe in the incarnation of the beloved Son, sent not to condemn but to save. The New Testament is composed of documents of various origins, having come from different cultural contexts, revealing diverse experiences. All agree, however, that the God of Jesus (sharing in God's triumph) is the very one who created the world.

Behind the covenant of Calvary, there is the covenant of Sinai, behind the covenant of Sinai stands the covenant with Noah. The Incarnation comes to confer on that covenant an undreamt-of fullness. It is not by chance that the letter to the Colossians, the letter to the Corinthians (1 Cor 8:6), the letter to the Hebrews, the Gospel of John, associate creation with Christ (as Son or as Word). Moreover, the incarnate Son, when he announces to his followers the persecutions that await them, always does so in a climate of hope. I confess that it is this climate that makes me of one mind with the proud protestation of Yossel Rakover: "You will not make me fall. . . . I will always believe in you, I will always love you despite yourself." I add: "If you give me the grace for it." For as a Christian, it is impossible for me not to connect this hope with "my God, my God, why have you forsaken me," which leads to the Resurrection. There for the Christian is the crux of the faithfulness of God with the martyrdom of those who are his. Yossel Rakover connects it to the vocation and the fate of the servant people of YHWH. I connect it to the vocation and fate of Jesus, the Servant of the Father, as the first community calls him (Acts 3:13, 26; 4:27, 30).

But the question remains—haunting. Why do you impel us on the Way of the Cross? One thinks of Job, obviously. Is there a response? I do not think so. It is within the secret of God, who has not revealed it.

In order to understand this, not to allow faith to be shattered, is not a strong inwardness necessary?

There you touch on a very important point. I have all but spoken of it, in evoking the errors of our Churches. I did not do so for fear of being unjust. But without playing the part of a critic, I believe that there is presently in the Catholic Church and elsewhere a crisis of inwardness, of spiritual emptiness. I do not know how to describe it. I would say that many people no longer venture inward where, on the one hand, they meet themselves and where, on the other hand, everything that emanates from existence settles, awaiting clarification. There is the fear of silence. We need "background music" everywhere. When in the liturgy there comes a moment of silence, one guesses, by the eyes and the gestures of those present, that it is empty. Because one does not know with which words to fill it, one thinks it is of no use. It is a pause, a breathing space. I copied out a sentence once, whose author I have forgotten and can no longer find. It evoked the intense silence that seizes the entire room at the moment when, the musicians being ready, the conductor of the orchestra prepares to lift the baton. A very dense silence, so that one could hear it. It is this quality of silence, which, before God, allows us to hear, to come alive. From the earliest days of my Christian education I have kept a keen sense of the need "to put on the presence of God," according to the expression in a prayer composed by Fénelon. How is this possible without silence? If the monasteries are places where this presence of God is more obvious than elsewhere, is it not because of their silence? From where does Gregorian chant draw its force, if not from this silence from which it is never separated: Its notes come out of this silence and they return to it.

During recent decades, a return to spirituality has characterized several Catholic contexts. Some contemplative communities of a different type from the monastic orders have been born, and several have survived. But they are still fragile growths. Many draw their inspiration from the charismatic movement. In regard to them my feelings have always wavered between a great sympathy and a difficulty. The sympathy comes from the fervor which is recognized there and from the thirst for prayer which that fervor arouses. My difficulty comes from a certain "enthusiasm," too exteriorized, too "Pentecostal," which is, however, quite moderated. Is there enough of this silence of which I spoke? In any case, it is obvious that these renewals are the sign that in the wounded Body of the Church, life still pulses. Certain of the "new communities"—Bosé occurs to me, for example—are high places of hope, of authentic buds of spring.

I wish to add a remark, in no way original, to what I have said about the crisis of inwardness. Inwardness is inseparable from the religious dimension of the person. The success of the sects, the appeal of the "spiritualists," some rather esoteric, the fashion of Buddhism and of Eastern techniques of concentration, justly make us anxious. But it is important to read the message there: in spite of everything, human persons remain religious, open to that which is able to respond to their need. They are awaiting someone who provides enlightenment.

Today, there is especially talk of meeting Christ in action, the welcoming of the other.

Yes, one need not oppose inwardness and engagement, not either . . . or, but both . . . and (kai . . . kai). The New Testament itself makes the connection between the generous gesture and meeting Christ. It is sufficient to remember Jesus' statement on welcoming the child (Matt 18:5) and especially the important passage on the Last Judgment. When kindness is shown to the hungry, the sick, the prisoner, the scorned, Christ is himself served. These are essential affirmations that have always inspired the Christian life. It is necessary that inwardness and engagement mutually enrich each other. I am thinking of the way of life of the Petits Frères and Petites Soeurs of the Gospel and the Petits Frères and Petites Soeurs of Jesus, two branches—which I knew very well and deeply love—of the family of Charles de Foucauld. I am thinking also about Madeleine Delbrêl, "who knows how to discover God in the noise of the street just as well as in the silence of a monastery because she knew how to make in herself some hollows of silence" (*Nous autres, gens des rues*, Postscript, p. 323). I think of Father Loew.

By chance I read in the newspaper *Le Monde* (February 18, 2000) an article concerning that complex man, the French socialist Jean Jaurès, philosopher, politician, and militant, holder of the *agregation* (certificate) of philosophy, haunted by the spiritual, colleague of Bergeon, held in contempt by Péguy. I found there this quotation: "True believers are those who wish to abolish the exploitation of man by man and, therefore, the hatred of man toward man, the hatred also of race toward race, of nation toward nation, all hatred, and truly create a humanity yet to exist. But to create humanity is to create reason, gentleness, love, and who knows if God is not at the basis of these things?" In this remarkable thought, Jaurès put the vision of God ("the clarity of God," "the soft light of Jesus" as he writes elsewhere)—in a rather pantheistic perspective—at the end of generosity, of altruistic acts. The Gospel puts God at the outset. But it never separates the attention to God from the creation of "a humanity yet to exist," the humanity God wills.

You speak of a Church wounded but not dying. You invoke forces of revival. What are the aspects of the Church that need healing?

Yossel Rakover's question, which resonates among Christians, forces us not only to examine, as I did, our responsibilities and mitigating circumstances, to call ourselves into question. It forces us, if we are serious and determined not to give up, to ask ourselves what in the Church of God must be revived or healed along the lines John XXIII had in mind when he convened the council. Cardinal Newman thought that at least a century was necessary for a council to bear fruit. What I call the Church's "wound" is an invitation to scrutinize that which is still not fully permeated by the vigor of Vatican II. I was thinking about it while looking at John Paul II in Cairo, exhausted by fatigue, collecting all his energies and his courage to repeat that there is no time to lose in the search for a new way to exercise the primacy of Rome. I have often said that the council has not ended as long as it is not yet "received." Its forces of revival are still in the flesh of the Church. They are at several levels, which I will very quickly examine with your help.

Are you able to clarify for us a point which surprises the faithful: bishops and priests have questions about themselves.

A little while ago, at the time of a meeting of bishops preparing for the synod in Rome, one of the bishops asked me: Explain to us what it is about our mission that is formally of the Gospel, which distinguishes us from being simple administrators of sacred things, from being simple guardians of ecclesial institutions.

When, returning to the Scripture, one seeks the roots of the term *episkopos,* one finds that which is connected to the larger theme of God's visitation. He approaches his own in order to achieve his design in their midst. In the *Benedictus,* Luke recognizes God's supreme visitation in the coming of Christ Jesus, the definitive encounter of humanity and God. To visit is *episkopein.* The bishop is, in his local church, the one charged with keeping this church in the larger grace of God's visitation made in Christ. He watches over it, but in order that this supreme and definitive visitation of God may continue for everyone. It is the bishop's mission to do what is needed so that this church continues to realize the Good News. All the bishop's tasks and responsibilities are united around this axis.

The presbyters are there to assist him in this task, especially when the bishop entrusts to them the responsibility of a parish community. Today many of these presbyters live in a serious identity crisis. The alarming drop in the number of ordinations to the presbyterate, leading to the growing number of parishes without a full-time priest, means that priests gradually lose every possibility for full involvement in a community. They are reduced to going from parish to parish to celebrate the Sunday Eucharist, their ministry often reduced to the celebration of the sacraments. Vatican II, however, had wanted something quite different: Around the Eucharistic synaxis would radiate all acts aiming at "the formation of an authentic Christian community" (*Presbyterorum ordinis* 6) with education in the faith, personal relations, care of the sick and poor, participation in the difficulties and joys of the human context. Moreover, often to favor the laity, in some settings certain functions have been unnecessarily removed from the presbyters which are normally theirs, as (in several dioceses) the celebration of baptism. A disappointed young priest said to me: "I simply do what a layperson is not able to do; I am reduced to being a minister of transubstantiation; I am no longer a pastor called to be the sign of Christ's presence to his own in the midst of adversities, needs, the great passages of life." In this situation, it is right that the priest (the presbyter), in his communion with his bishop, is ordained: to make present, both in the presidency of the Eucharist and in daily acts of the "care of souls" or of mercy, the one of whom the Gospel texts tell us that he [Christ] was moved in the face of their misery, "because they were as sheep without a shepherd." The parish priest and vicar are pastors quite as much by their heart as by the sacraments over which they preside. Many Christians would be able to attest how meeting with a priest of the Gospel changed their lives: the visitation of God in Jesus Christ. There are also deacons. I wonder if a ministry is given to these ordained persons that is truly theirs. They have often been made mini-priests, filling the void left by the lack of ordinations to the priesthood. Now they are, in the great tradition, the link between the Eucharist and the ministry of charity, especially for the most deprived and those most greatly ridiculed. I know a deacon in Paris, the brother of one of my best friends, who knew how to transform lives in this way . . .

What is a local church?

It is only to be understood in the function of God's visitation made in Jesus Christ. It is the human space—with all the realism of its history, its problems, its projects, its culture, its joys, and its pains—linking its inhabitants in a community of destiny and where the Gospel has taken root. The human community thus becomes communion, communion of these baptized people among themselves, communion with all the other communities scattered throughout the world and where the Gospel has brought forth its fruits. In it the visitation of Christ continues.

The preaching of the Word is, in itself, the memory of what in Jesus Christ God accomplished in the days of his visitation. The celebration of the eucharistic synaxis is the sacramental memorial of the Easter event where this visit culminates. In the care of the poor, of life's wounded, of the sick, of the marginalized, the love manifested by God, when in his Son he visited suffering humanity, is made present. Engagement for the sake of peace, justice, and law is the echo of Jesus' teaching at the time of his visitation. In short, the local church, focused in the celebration of the Eucharist, is nothing other than the fruit, today and in this part of the universe, of what we praise in the liturgy as the act of God's agape, accomplished "once and for all" for all human beings of every time and of every place.

The Church of God is the communion of all these local churches. Already present in God, in its head, the resurrected Christ, it thus takes form in the flesh of the people and in the realism of the human condition. It seems to me—and I have written it time and again—that its depth is revealed to us in the wonderful second chapter of the letter to the Ephesians, listed in the Pauline corpus. The anonymous author places the Church at the precise point where, in the Cross of Christ, the two hostile parts of humanity, divided by religious reasons, are reconciled "in a single body." There the text adds: "He has put to death hostility." When I say that the local church is planted most deeply in the human condition, I am thinking above all else about this. For since my studies in philosophy, preparing my doctorate, I have been struck by the power of hatred. It is everywhere, even in families. Now the local church is the human community where those who normally abhor each other celebrate together the eucharistic synaxis. To the Pauline list—Jew-Greek, slave-free, man-woman, civilized-barbarian, circumcised-uncircumcised—are added century after century many hostile pairings. I have very often recounted my emotion when, at the very depths of the war which set their country ablaze, a Hutu and a Tutsi, after having exchanged the kiss of peace with each other, came side by side to take communion, tears in their eyes: the brother of the Hutu had just been assassinated by the Tutsis. Why have all the Catholics of that country not done as much, I am sometimes asked when I refer to this episode. Very simply because, baptized without being adequately evangelized, they have not understood what the Church of God is, a Church which is nothing abstract but which is realized in concrete places of humanity, places harrowed by the atrocious problem of hatred. It is easy for me to declare my love for the Scythian or the barbarian who is at a distance; it is difficult for me to love the Scythian or the barbarian who is my neighbor. Our membership in the same local church is what constrains me. Is it not the place of Christ's visitation?

But this raises the question of ecumenism . . .

The division of Christians is for me probably the greatest scandal of the Church's history. I am convinced that it is, much more than the vices or mistakes of our societies, the great obstacle to evangelization. I see there the mark par excellence of the power of the Evil One, whom the scriptural texts call the Adversary.

It is extremely serious that men and women who proclaim to have found in Christ the answer to their search for faithfulness, who confess the supreme faith of agape for God and for "the brethren," who have been baptized in the Easter power of the Cross where God destroys hatred, turn their communities into enemy camps. I say "enemy." I could say, in referring to the historical documents which I have examined at length, groups "in a state of hostility." I have just been rereading some of the documents of the Reformation and Counter-Reformation. They are hardly enlightening. Certainly, there is only one truth, and Paul himself, not to mention the Johannine writings, is harsh toward those who depart from it. I also know that, as the Council of Chalcedon proves, the sometimes violent confrontation of viewpoints—Cyril of Alexandria was not very gentle!—can allow for essential clarifications.

But today the situation of the Churches is no longer quite the same. We have attained a certitude that on fundamental points of faith we are in a real communion, although it is imperfect, at least in relation to the major Churches. To that, the conviction is added, although rarely explained, that very often our attachment to our confessional differences comes more from a fear of losing our identity than from a deep interest in the truth. The experience—slow but fruitful—of the Lutheran-Catholic dialogue has just shown us how honest and humble research, on both sides, is able to pull down age-old walls of polemic and division. Since its creation ARCIC—the Anglican-Roman Catholic International Commission—has had the same experience. Diversity is able to appear as a richness. When will we cease to see there a difference that divides?

Of all the Churches, the Catholic Church is the one today whose commitment to the service of unity is probably the most conscious and courageous. In the great beginning made by John XXIII, then in the

Decree on Ecumenism, Paul VI and John Paul II have understood the seriousness of Christ's wish, *Ut unum sint*. In this record, several of their texts and actions will remain among the most beautiful of recent decades. I am thinking about the gesture of Paul VI kissing the feet of the representative of the patriarch of Constantinople, of the deeply moving photograph of the aged John Paul II surrounded by the delegates of Patriarch Bartholomeus and the archbishop of Canterbury before the Holy Door of the basilica of St. Paul-Outside-the-Walls. I am thinking also about the courage with which, in spite of the lack of enthusiastic responses, John Paul II has not ceased to call the Eastern Churches to resume full communion. Or again of his plan to visit the dying patriarch of Armenia. These are not moves of pure politeness. Paul VI and John Paul II have been foremost witnesses to the movement of the Spirit pushing the Churches to break with the abominable scandal of division.

But let us return to the local church: the laity.

It was long ago that Leo XIII himself wrote that the role of the faithful is reduced to a single duty: to accept the teachings that are given to them, to conform their conduct to these teachings, to assist the Church's intentions. The Code of 1983, repeating lines of *Lumen gentium* that had disturbed several bishops, states that the duty of the laity is sometimes to give their opinion to their pastors on matters that concern the well-being of the Church and to make that opinion known to other Christians. Moreover, the laity are more and more closely associated with even "pastoral" tasks. I know parishes without a resident pastor that survive only thanks to laypeople who, in connection with the bishop, take charge of catechesis, prayer, and several times a month, the Sunday gathering. This is very good.

May I be allowed to express a worry: it may well happen that these laity become clericalized, or even that they may clericalize themselves. I know that this is very frequently the result of the abnormal situation that the scarcity of ordained ministers creates. This is why I make no accusations. Especially in view of the future, however, it is advisable to be clear in a world where the values of the Gospel are rudely mistreated. It is not in quasi-clerical functions, but in very concrete tasks of what is called "the temporal order" that the laity are destined to live their Christian vocation, fully exercising there their responsibility. Profession, trade, political commitment, cultural institutions, educational jobs, family life—such are moreover the human arenas where the confrontation between lofty principles of the Gospel and customary behaviors are most bitter. Laity in their local churches are partners with God the Creator in working at the construction and healing of what Vatican II calls "the temporal order" (*Apostolicam actuositatem* 7), to make of it the world God wishes. Certain very tightly packed expressions of the Decree on the Apostolate of the Laity have been forgotten. These expressions stress that the mission of the Church is not limited to carrying to the world the Word of Christ and his grace, but that it also wills, by the Spirit of the Gospel, to penetrate and perfect "the temporal order" (5). They add that the laity, inseparably members of the Church and members of the human City, have only one conscience, their Christian conscience, which guides them in their temporal commitment. Just as I am struck by the scarcity of vocations to the ministry, so I am struck by how scarce the voices of Christian laity become in the great debates that disturb our societies. Now it matters more and more—when the voices of Church leaders are rarely heeded—that active laity, truly aware of the problems and firm in their convictions, express themselves on the public stage and in the media. If they are silent, who will cause the voice of the Gospel to be heard? And within the ecclesial community, if the laity in the diversity of their viewpoints are not heard or do not make themselves heard on the ever more complex political, economic, social, and educational questions, the Church runs the risk of being directed down blind alleys. A true dialogue with serious laity seems to me more and more the only means of avoiding harmful polarizations.

This obviously requires that the laity be instructed about the great truths of the faith, informed about the directions of the Church. Much effort has been deployed to this end. But I do not believe that it has been adequate. Numerous laity have found in the *Catechism of the Catholic Church* the instrument of knowledge that they were lacking. It is necessary to give thanks for this. But how many times have I been asked to explain a certain chapter, judged to be very difficult? Our Christian communities know less and less about the very bases of the givens of the faith.

I react against the "clericalization" of the laity. I think, however, that in their commitment to the service of sacramental and pastoral life, a "declericalization" of the local churches takes shape. Let me be quite clear here, for often on this point my thought has been entirely misconstrued. I am among those who believe in the necessity of an ordained

ministry, that of the bishop, of the presbyter, and of the deacon. This necessity cannot be relativized. But, on the one hand, it is necessary to
reestablish for the laity certain functions to which their baptismal grace
entitles them and which have been co-opted by the "clergy." On the
other hand, it will be necessary in upcoming decades—still of course in
communion with the bishop—to create new community "services" or
ministries under the responsibility of the laity. The list of ministries will
probably not be exactly what we know today. A rather considerable evolution has begun under our eyes and the needs of the time are perhaps,
from God's viewpoint, the providential occasion better to adapt the
Churches to the problems still to come. Therefore I pass a twofold judgment on the engagement of the laity in pastoral life. On the one hand, I
say: Look out, don't create pseudo-clerics, avoid reducing the mission of
the presbyters in order to exalt the role of the laity. On the other hand I
say: Don't simply make them supply pastors for our hard times. Make of
them building blocks of a new ministerial pattern around the bishop, his
presbyters, and his deacons. My ecumenical work has put me in contact
with Churches having mostly undiversified ministries. I have noted
there a great lack of attention to the needs of several categories of people.
Now, according to its tradition, the Catholic Church rejects that anyone
be deprived of what represents for it a service of Christ's presence in
every depth of human need. For the Catholic Church, this is a call for
new ministries, clarifying what was formerly the role of the priest.

In the local church, there are also men and women religious. They
are more and more forgotten, no doubt because their recruitment has
fallen off. Perhaps they have spoken too much about perfection, and
not enough about goodness. For Christ has come to free the profound
goodness of humanity, which evil cannot devour. Goodness exists; evil
is not destined to have the final word. The Church is charged by the
Spirit to dream, to awaken, to release the goodness that sleeps in the
human heart.

This describes the project of the religious life. It aims to free the
profound goodness of the person and to bear witness to it for God. In
effect, when religious men and women reflect on their life, they quickly
become aware of that for which their faithfulness is a struggle, so that,
in their own hearts, the dividing line between good and evil shifts in
favor of the good. They seek to live together in such a way that, in spite
of everything, goodness triumphs in them, in their communal existence,
in their action. Their goal is to become good, for the sake of God and
his Gospel, to spread this goodness. Poverty, chastity, and obedience

have this objective. To seek the "perfection of the Gospel" is to seek goodness that pervades from all sides the visitation of God in Christ.

It seems to me that we do not emphasize enough everything the religious communities accomplish all around us in the service of this goodness. Mother Teresa or Sister Emmanuelle only serve to give more radiance to a form of life which a great many religious men and women lead with faith, courage, and love all over the world. I am thinking about women religious in charge of a home for AIDS patients; about a congregation having transformed its infirmary into a clinic for palliative treatment; about Latin American sisters active with women of the *favellas;* about the Congregation of Spiritians of Madagascar welcoming and educating the "children of the street." I have thought and written that such communities are today in the full flower of the Gospel, even while they are in acute distress because the lack of vocations has forced them to close institutions in which they had placed their hope. Perhaps they are even more faithful to the call of God than formerly. Their intentions have slowly shifted from observance, sincere and courageous, to the quality of the heart. They have allowed themselves to be conquered by the goodness which the sick of Galilee perceived in Christ.

What are the great axes of the life of a local church thus conceived?

It is obvious that a local church is not able to live if it is not nourished by the Word of God and constantly sent back to this Word. This Word has in it the memory of what God has revealed of himself and accomplished. Since its beginnings, this Word has been given to the Church in various ways, each of which has its specificity and its purpose: preaching, catechesis, theological teaching, homily. A Church that no longer hears the Word or which contents itself with substitutes is dying. But it is not enough to listen; it is necessary to understand. Thus the importance of the homily, of preaching.

In several countries preaching is currently in crisis. The reason is not only the weariness of the ministers having to celebrate several Masses: when I preach at four Eucharists, my fourth sermon is usually less than dynamic. The reason for this situation is more profound. For some twenty years, the research of the exegetes and the theologians into the tension between the historical Jesus and the Christ of faith has been very closely combined with the media's interest in religious fact. Newspaper or magazine articles, television and radio news flashes increase. Religious information, ordinarily poorly checked and often quite tendentious, is delivered to all, including the faithful and their pastors. An encompassing blur has thus gradually come to surround the person of Jesus and the texts of the Gospels. Pastors are getting to the point of no longer knowing what to say in certain situations, of no longer daring to comment on several passages of the Gospels that deal with the life of Jesus or the words placed on his lips. In order to say something that is wise and useful, they then speak about social questions. Preaching takes refuge in ethical teaching. It no longer dares to touch on certain chapters of dogma. Confronted with such honest silence, fundamentalist groups appear, vigorously propounding a reading that makes little intelligent sense and further damages the truth. Such a situation is serious, and it will very soon be necessary to confront it by a serious reflection on the nature of the faith and its relation to historical sources. Revelation exists only as historically received, without being identified with history. Even if they brush against each other, the formal object of faith and that of historical study are not one and the same. It is impossible to know Christ without knowing what the Gospels say about Jesus, son of Mary. But it is just as impossible to know what Jesus truly was without seeking to uncover what the Resurrection evokes as a movement from intuition to explicit affirmation.

This is one of the spheres where different Christian confessions, all confronted by the same problem, must work together. Admittedly without success, I have tried to get it on the agenda of the Commission on Faith and Order in its program on "Confessing the Apostolic Faith," for which I am responsible. People do not seem to understand, especially in the Protestant context—this is quite surprising—the importance of an in-depth study of the faith that justifies and continues to keep the Christian in the reality of salvation. The fine agreement between Lutherans and Catholics on justification, however, should open the way to a common deepening of the bond of the faith with the truth of the history where God reveals himself, this truth which the Word transmits.

The moment when the local church expresses itself in its most profound reality and returns to its roots is the Sunday eucharistic synaxis. The current crisis of vocation in ministry has had at least the positive consequence of forcing parishes to have only one Sunday Mass, bringing them together in one single celebration of the Lord's Passover.

At the synaxis—that is to say at the eucharistic assembly—all the baptized of the community receive, after having praised God, the single and indivisible Body of Christ, in which they are one. According to a fine expression of Saint Augustine, they are, individually and all together, what they receive. The repentant sinners and the holy persons who have to reproach themselves only for peccadillos, the minister and the laity seated in the last pew, the rich who help the Church with their wealth and the poor whom the Church assists by giving alms, the politician and the undocumented refugee, all are thus caught up in the power of the Easter agape that is the "mystery of unity." Cyril of Alexandria used to say that they are melted into unity. It is this unity that forms out of their acts of thanksgiving and intercession a single and indivisible thanksgiving, a single and indivisible intercession.

This is a point on which I have continued to insist. From the beginning, the eucharistic synaxis has had among its constitutive elements the care of the poor, of widows, of prisoners, of refugees, of life's wounded; quite different matters than the slightly artificial references in our general prayers. Around 150, St. Justin wrote a description of the Sunday Eucharist, close in its structure to our current synaxis. He indicates how the gifts each person brings, by being presented to the assembly, are shared with those women and men who are in need. Throughout the entire tradition, multiple witnesses remind us of this dimension of the synaxis. The explanation is not simply that someone takes advantage of the assembly of the whole community to request its generosity. The reason is infinitely deeper. The Eucharist is the memorial of the event where God bound into the unity of the Body of Christ members of a humanity torn apart by wealth and exclusion. In this unity only the law of sharing can rule, for there is but one Body of Christ: it is necessary then to abolish the distance between rich and poor, powerful and weak.

Times have changed. Charity as practiced in previous centuries would scarcely make sense today. We must count on society's laws. Nevertheless, it appears to me necessary to revive in our Churches this connection between the eucharistic synaxis and the realization of each person's responsibility in the face of human distress and misery in the entire world, but in a particular manner in the area that constitutes the local church. The Orthodox speak of "the liturgy after the liturgy," a liturgy of charity after the Liturgy of the Eucharist, a liturgy of the Body of Christ, suffering in its wretched members, after the liturgy of the Body of the glorified Christ. Those whom we call "practicing" Christians are so in truth only when the practice of charity comes to be grafted onto sacramental practice. In the past, religious communities usually made this connection between the service of God and the service of the poor in the local church. They are disappearing. It would be very serious if this relation that makes such a Church fully eucharistic disappears with them, especially when new miseries, both material and spiritual, are being born.

Why this stress on the Eucharist as memorial?

I believe that one of the great graces that God has given in our century through theology has been the rediscovery of the Eucharist as the Passover Memorial. It has been at the juncture of ecumenical dialogue with biblical, patristic, and liturgical renewal. Around this rediscovery, important agreements have been reached between Christian confessions that were formerly prisoners to sterile polemics. Far from diminishing the grandeur of the Lord's sacrament, it has exalted it.

What in fact is the Eucharist? It is the act by which God the Father, answering the plea of the community assembled before him, sends the Holy Spirit so that the bread and the cup of wine become in truth the Body and Blood of the resurrected Lord, truly given as Bread of Life and a new covenant. The great event of the Passover, where Christ Jesus gives himself to the Father for the salvation of all humanity, thus becomes present and efficacious for this portion of humanity, the community assembled in this place. When the community, in thanks and supplication, recalls to the Father the miracle of the gift of his Son and the Son's shattering acceptance of the Cross, leading to the Resurrection, the Spirit makes it as if it were contemporaneous with the Easter event, in that historical time and in that place on the world map. The wall of time separating the historical today and the time of the Passover of Christ is, as it were, broken down. It is not therefore a question of a simple memory of a purely commemorative image. It is a question of a true meeting with the event of salvation, which for God—the one who in his eternity transcends all times and places—is still present in an eternal today. The community thus really and truly receives, under the signs of the sacrament, the Body and Blood of the sacrifice, glorified at the Resurrection.

We sense the importance of this meeting between the local church, immersed in the this-worldly problems that characterize its faithful, and the Passover Event, present in all its truth and salvific power. I have often said that here there is somehow no longer any distance between the community and God's mercy. The community is like the Good Thief: looking away from its own merit, entirely riveted on God's gift which unites it sacramentally, despite its sin.

The community likewise knows itself to be in communion with all the other local churches scattered in time and space. They also are sacramentally united by the same event. Even more—this seems to me crucial—it knows itself to be in communion with all those who, since the Jewish Passover, have been seated and still sit around the paschal meal, and it is with them that the community proclaims in the anamnesis "we await your coming in glory."

It is my conviction that Jesus' last meal before the Cross was probably not the paschal meal but a fraternal meal, celebrated in the atmosphere of the Passover festival. But the Church has seen it as the resumption, in the mystery of Christ, of the meaning and of the profound role that the paschal meal had for Jewish awareness. At the moment when the holy people were lifting up their praise to God while crying out their hope—"make present your day and the time of your grace"—God, in the Passover of Christ, the long-awaited Paschal Lamb, was fulfilling his promise. In his Messiah he caused the Day of Salvation to shine forth, remembered in the Sunday Eucharist which is the sacramental memorial. Nevertheless, everything is not yet finished. Paul says to the Corinthians that one is still waiting for "the end, when Christ will return the kingdom to God the Father, after having destroyed every rule, every authority, every power. . . . But when it says that all has been subjected, this does not include the One who has subjected all to him. When all things will have been subjected to him, then the Son himself will be subjected to the one who has subjected all to him in order that God may be everything to everyone." Now it is this end, this accomplished Day that Christians await, in communion with the Jewish people. United in the event which begins what is called the history of salvation, the Exodus, whose annual memorial *(zikkaron)* is the pascal meal, we also await the final completion, the Parousia of the Lord, who will usher in the great eschatological banquet "with Abraham, Isaac and Jacob" in the kingdom. Thus it is that at each eucharistic synaxis the memory both of the meal at the Exodus and the still-awaited Banquet is celebrated. In the eucharistic memorial, I hear below the surface the words of Paul to the Romans: "the hardening of a part of Israel will last until the full number of the Gentiles have entered, and thus all Israel will be saved. . . . From the point of view of the election, they are loved, for the sake of the fathers; for the gifts and the call of God are irrevocable . . . ; they have disobeyed in order that, as a result of the mercy exercised toward you, they may obtain mercy in turn." The synaxis of the local church finds here its place and its importance.

I have recalled the tension between the *already* of salvation that shines in the resurrection and the final Day of the Parousia of the Lord Christ. The engagement of the Church of God for the kingdom "which is and which is to come" is encompassed there. Christ returns to the members of his Body, inseparable from their head and carriers of his Spirit, to cooperate with God not only in the proclamation of the Gospel to the ends of the earth, but also in the destruction of "every dominion, every power," all the forces of evil, all the lies of the Enemy. In the bread and the memorial cup, the community receives its Lord exactly in this situation of waiting, where the grace offered to all humanity germinates and comes to fruit in this time which is "the time of the Church." The Church is united in Christ in the expectation of its final Day, "until he comes." Each synaxis thus places the Church again before its mission and its faithfulness to its task. Obviously, the laity here are again the first to be implicated. After the Sunday synaxis, I often wonder how conscious we are of this judgment from God, confronting all present. I never leave the synaxis unscathed. Not only, if the homily has been well done, have I been examined by the Word of God, but also the reception of the Lord's Body and Blood has planted in me a demand: to be, where I live, an architect of the transformation of this world into the world which God wishes, a world where the Gospel is the law, where there is no need to be known as the bearer of particular charisms or to hold an important place in society. It suffices to be baptized, to do with an evangelical spirit the duty to which life itself has bound me. If I am a mother of a family, to be in this evermore maltreated cell of the Church a teacher of humanity according to God. If I am a journalist, to be in the world of media a person professionally competent and seeking the truth without compromise. If I am a builder, to be a conscientious worker, a witness to justice and to respect for others in my work environment. If I am a nurse, to be an instrument of God's tenderness with the sick and not simply a technical agent.

You say that the local church is open to other Churches? How is it open?

I have been deeply misunderstood on this point, or perhaps there is pleasure in attributing to me a vision that is not mine. Some editors of ecclesiastical journals are happy to create scandals. I have never said or written that the Church of God comes about from the sum or addition of local churches. I have always affirmed, thousands of times, the contrary. I make a quite different point: that the Church of God is the communion (the *koinonia*) of local churches that exist, have existed, or will exist. I explain that there is only one faith, indivisible, that of the Church presented by the admirable letter to the Ephesians; one single baptism, that of the Church presented by the letter to the Ephesians; one single Eucharist, that of the Church presented by the letter to the Ephesians; one single apostolic ministry, that of the Church presented by the letter to the Ephesians. There is this single faith, this single baptism, this single Eucharist, this single ministry which the Spirit offers to the human community of Corinth, of Rome, of Lyons, of Milan, of Ottawa, of Harare and which, accepted by them, makes them Churches. By this faith, this baptism, this Eucharist, this ministry, all indivisible, these Churches are among themselves in *communion*. The Church of God on this earth, *hic et nunc*, is this *communion* of local churches in the unique and indivisible gift of the Spirit, and the Church of God in history is the *communion* of all local churches, lifted up by the Spirit, which have been, are, and will be until the Parousia of the Lord. All the locales of humanity, with the concreteness of their problems and the specificity of their particular features, are seized by the salvific power of the Cross, which "assembles" them in God, while respecting their diversity, a diversity derived largely from the created order. Humanity is saved not simply because its individuals are, but also because the communities which make it up are, as it were, clasped in the power of the Gospel.

And what is to be said about episcopal collegiality and the ministry of the Bishop of Rome?

Since the local churches are in communion, the bishops who have responsibility to keep them in the grace of the visitation of Christ are also in communion. To express this communion of bishops, the Second Vatican Council used a term borrowed from Saint Cyprian (around 250) and thus not a New Testament term: the word "college." Some people would have preferred the word "fraternity," but the question was so hotly debated in the council that they did not linger to discuss vocabulary. In effect, the stakes were elsewhere. It was a question of completing the work of the First Vatican Council, interrupted by war without being able to finish its reflections on the episcopate. In particular, the declarations on the primacy of the Bishop of Rome had not been extended into an elaboration of the role of bishops.

At Vatican II the debates were tense and difficult. Indeed, since 1870, the Roman primacy had filled the horizon and the Catholic

Church, firmly attached to the Bishop of Rome as its supreme head, had very often underrated or forgotten the bishops. In spite of the approval by Pius IX of the "elaboration" of the German episcopate, declaring that such was not the intention of the council, the bishops were ordinarily considered, and they themselves often acted, more as subalterns than as genuine leaders of their local churches. Primacy had, as it were, banished the episcopate into obscurity. Vatican II proposed to correct this anomaly that several persons continued to regard as untouchable. This was accomplished by recalling that the Church of God has only one leader, one single head *(Kephale)*, Christ Jesus. During his earthly life, however, Christ assembled a group of men whom he charged, as a group, after his resurrection to function as witnesses and ministers of the Gospel. Strictly speaking, this group could not have successors, since at the heart of its mission was its role as witness. The Twelve were those who had recognized in the Resurrected the one with whom they had lived and whom they had followed until his death. Founded on this unique witness, however, the college of bishops since the time of the apostles has been the group of ministers whom the Spirit has charged to relay the apostles' mission.

A person becomes a bishop by being assumed into this college and thus enrolled in its solidarity and unity, which guarantee that a single and identical Gospel is preached throughout the world; an identical baptism and an identical Eucharist are celebrated in spite of the diversity of places and situations. The bishop receives a special gift of the Spirit for the specific mission of "assembling in unity scattered children," through a unique and united service of the resurrected Lord. Wherever the Spirit is given, it creates unity, even among ministers. The Spirit is thus the one who binds together, through the grace of ordination, the episcopal college.

It is in the midst of this college and in the service of this unity brought about by the Spirit that one of the bishops, that of Rome, has a special role connected to that of Peter: "Strengthen your brothers in the faith." Rome has a very particular importance because of the martyrdom there of Peter and Paul; Peter who connects the Church to its roots in the Old Testament, Paul who connects it to the universality of peoples. From this fact, the Bishop of Rome is the one among his brother bishops who is charged with seeing that they never stray from the apostolic witness, grasped in all its depth and fullness. Rereading a few days ago the bulls of Paul III, Julius III, and Paul IV concerning the Council of Trent, I am struck anew by this association with Peter and

Paul to establish the authority of primacy. I am equally impressed by the remark of John Paul II, reported in a work on his contact with Africa (C. Sliwinski, "John Paul II in Africa," in Wierbianski, *The Shepherd for All People*), and quoted in the biography by G. Weigel, *Witness to Hope: The Biography of John Paul II*, p. 374).

He indirectly addressed his detractors in Italy:

> Some people think that the Pope should not travel so much. That he should stay in Rome, as before. I often hear such advice, or read it in newspapers. But the local people here say, "Thank God you came here, for you can only learn about us by coming. How could you be our pastor without knowing us? Without knowing who we are, how we live, what is the historical moment we are going through?" This confirms me in the belief that it is time for the Bishops of Rome . . . to become successors not only of Peter but also of St. Paul, who, as we know, could never sit still and was constantly on the move.

We also remember the attachment of Paul VI to the figure of the Apostle of the nations. It seems to me that in the upcoming decades, without necessarily making himself a pilgrim, the Bishop of Rome will increasingly need to be the confidant, the support of his fellow bishops in the rough confrontation between the Gospel and the movements of ideas in society. Primacy is exercised by the heart more than by commands. I know that the Pastoral Letters of the New Testament are not by Paul. But their style seems to me to be a model for the Pauline face of the ministry of the Bishop of Rome. It is what many bishops leaving for their *ad limina* visits expect to find in their meeting with the Primate. This is important. They wish to be understood, not judged, one of them said to me.

But since they are together a college, a "fraternity," it is also in their dialogue among themselves, especially within a region, that the bishops have to seek and to find what they need for their ministry. I have the impression that, apart from the meetings of the episcopal conference, the (horizontal) dialogue among the bishops has lost the excitement of the first years after the council. It may be that I am wrong, but the institutional seems to prevail over the "heartfelt." Several bishops are tempted to give their (vertical) relation to Rome priority over their fraternal relations with bishops of the same region. Now the law of collegiality is that these two relations, the vertical and the horizontal, are equally honored and realized. Both are necessary, and neither can marginalize the other. The health of catholicity depends on it.

I know how complex the question of episcopal conferences is. I have warned against a bureaucracy sometimes more cumbersome than that of the Roman Curia. But their importance cannot be rejected for that reason. They are not simply instruments for recording and broadcasting what comes "from on high." The bishops who make up the conferences are themselves also, each in his place and all of them together, *vicarius et legatus Christi*, the voice of Christ, the Good Shepherd. Their concerns but also their intuitions are as bound to him as are the concerns and intuitions—certainly more weighty and comprehensive—of the Primate. The Church of God being the *communion* of local churches, the care of Christ for the entire Church (the *catholica*) is actualized in the care of all these churches by their pastors. I do not believe that I am wrong nor that I fall (as I have been accused) into a semi-Gallican episcopalism in saying that there are wishes, suggestions of the Good Shepherd, which he addresses to the Primate himself by his brother bishops in local churches, all having received from the Spirit with the grace of their ordination the *sollicitudo totius Ecclesiae.* Are these brother bishops heard with the fervor with which they listen to the voice of the *primus servus servorum Dei*?

The Catholic tradition proclaims, with reason, the necessity of the primacy of the Bishop of Rome. In other Churches—as in certain Anglican groups—that have broken with primacy, the need for it can today be felt. It is obvious, as the two Vatican councils have firmly recalled, that the function of primacy extends beyond its relations with the other bishops. It has an impact on all the faithful. It is necessary therefore to avoid thinking of primacy simply as a kind of technical, inter-episcopal function, or as one theologian wrote, "a liaison office among bishops." It is also impossible to integrate it with a simple presidency, as that of the president of the World Alliance of Reformed Churches. The Orthodox understand it quite well. Primacy possesses at the core of the episcopal collegiality a symbolic function, which has emotional colors, expressed by the customary title, Holy Father. When Paul VI hesitated over possibly resigning, this symbolic dimension dissuaded him. He confided to Jean Guitton, "You do not resign from fatherhood." I have often wondered about the source of this undeniable feature of the papacy that the poor conduct of several popes is not sufficient to call into question. Then I am always sent back to the sympathetic and attractive figure of Simon Peter, whose vicar is the Bishop of Rome. There is clearly only one Father, the heavenly One, and it is rather surprising that Reformed thinkers believe it necessary to remind us of this, as if we had forgotten. But instructed by his own misery and his experience of sin, nevertheless charged by Christ to "feed" the lambs and sheep of the flock, the Peter of the Acts of the Apostles appears to me as an image of the father of the Prodigal Son, waiting and welcoming the children of God, to lead them to the banquet of the kingdom. Such is his attitude toward the Jews at Pentecost, with Cornelius, at the meeting in Jerusalem, no doubt also in his decision to eat with Gentiles, then shying away for fear of shocking the Jews. We recognize the mark of this goodness in John XXIII, which explains without a doubt why the few years of his pontificate were a turning point in how we look at the papacy. In the episcopal college, the Bishop of Rome has the function of signifying in a particular manner that which all his brother bishops serve, the goodness of God. Since he is the first, the one thought of first when one seeks the Church's thought and attitude, it falls to him to show the world that the Church is *sacramentum* of God's mercy. His very power of jurisdiction appears to me subordinated to his relation to the mercy of the God and the Father of the Lord Jesus Christ. This point is, to my mind, central.

The result of all this must not be that Catholics behave as if there were only one true bishop, forgetting that in the life of their local church they should first attend to their own bishop. He is neither a subordinate nor an auxiliary of the Bishop of Rome, but his colleague in the college. Too often during visits of the pope to their countries, they create the impression, stressed by the other Christian confessions, that "the pope is all they need." It is too much to speak of idolatry. It is nevertheless necessary to note that a cult of the papacy sometimes results in excesses.

In the last several months, some cardinals and bishops—Cardinals Koenig, Hume, Etchegarary, Martini, Archbishop Quinn, bishops of the synods of Asia and the Pacific—have spoken out on this subject. They are reacting against what they regard as a trend to set to the side the responsibility of the local bishops to the advantage of a Roman centralization. An Australian bishop thus described the malaise: "We have the impression that Rome no longer has confidence in us, she takes in hand questions which we have the competence and the capacity to handle by ourselves. Rome expresses its desires as wishes, which she dictates to us; she chokes the authority of the episcopal conferences." Several facts disclosed by the press support this judgment. It seems that, stricken by panic or dizzied by muddled situations weighted with consequences for the future, the Roman See takes over cases and handles them according to its own principles and points of view. But, our Australian bishop added, Rome lacks a realistic and nuanced knowledge of the context, expectations, and forces of reaction. Moreover, in wanting to act too quickly, one risks compromising everything. Unintentionally, Rome proves those right who locally undermine the authority and work of the bishops.

The problem is very complex, and at least since 1986–87 I have often expressed myself on this point. It is not necessarily a negation of the council on the part of Rome, but—as surprising as it may seem—of a certain reading which has resurfaced. *Lumen gentium* was not sufficiently clear on the relation between the Roman primacy and the episcopal college. It was clearly affirmed that the full, supreme, and universal power of the college exists only in communion with the Bishop of Rome, never apart from this communion. It has not been specified if the full, supreme, universal power of the Bishop of Rome can be exercised without a necessary relation to the episcopal college. Is the Primate able to act independently from the college? *Lumen gentium* says that he is always able to act "freely," without specifying what this "free" action implies. Everything is left to his personal sense of the duty of fraternal solidarity, to his respect for the vocation of his brother bishops, to his perception of certain exigencies that his brother bishops do not appear to perceive. The spirit of Vatican II is not comprehended in the letter of the text, because of the interventions of a council minority fearful of a devaluation of primacy and a democratization of the Church. The present confusion is one consequence of this.

What do you think of the Curia?

Around the Bishop of Rome is his Curia. He would not know how to function without it. It would be unjust and childish to make it the scapegoat for all the ills of the Church. I cry over all the rooftops that, without the Pontifical Council for Promoting Christian Unity (formerly the Secretariat for Unity), the Catholic Church never would have made its ecumenical breakthrough, the correspondence between Paul VI and Athenagoras never would have existed, the Lutheran-Catholic agreement on justification would never have seen the light of day. One can say as much about the Pontifical Council for Justice and Peace. But the Curia is a rather particular environment, a mingling of churchmen totally devoted to the Church and firmly attached to the spirit of Vatican II (I have met several of them at the Casa del Clero), of incompetent priests sent by their diocese, of *monsignori* "making a career." Moreover, especially since the pontificate of Pius XII, the Curia has acquired a certain consciousness of its importance and has created for itself a vocation less of a servant of the episcopal body than of "officer for the Church's faithfulness," leading it to check, regulate, and sometimes reprimand the bishops. A cardinal who knew the Curia well, and whom it feared, said to me that several of its influential members mistrusted the principles stemming from Vatican II and, without necessarily rejecting the council which they often quote, remained deeply attached to the "Church before John XXIII." It was the model. One thus understands that relations with local bishops, grappling with burning problems, are either warm or difficult according to the spirit of the prefect and secretary of this or that congregation, that episcopal conferences sometimes see their efforts disputed by clerics who know their language poorly and fail to see the nuances.

The desire for a serious reform of the Curia arises everywhere. People ask that it be an auxiliary of the Primate and not take over the bishops' functions, attentive to the evolution of societies, composed of persons truly competent in the fields for which they are responsible and capable of dialogue. Everyone who has called for this reform stresses that it must be more radical than those of Paul VI and John Paul II. One person (Archbishop Quinn) has even proposed a method. Let us confess that it will not be an easy thing. Change does not come easily for something which has behind it centuries of experience and traditions, handing on its methods from one person to another. The Roman See needs a Curia; without it, things today being what they are, the Primate clearly would not be able to accomplish fully his task. To return to an example I gave: how, without the Pontifical Council for Unity, would he be able to maintain his relations with other Christians, to evaluate the quality of dialogue, to think about the future, to organize his meetings with leaders of the Churches, to know what challenges to accept? To want the Curia to disappear, as some do, is very naive in the global context of the Catholic Church and in light of the function which the two Vatican councils have acknowledged for the Primate, placing him at the crux of local church relations.

Above all, it is proper to ask what is the authentic function of the Curia in a Church which, according to the spirit of Vatican II, respects with great seriousness the proper responsibility of the local bishops and refuses that all be centrally dictated. This center can no longer be understood according to the monarchical model. Christ did not make Peter a sovereign, and it is not by accident that the great tradition very early linked Paul to him as the source and explanation of the role of the Roman See. Paul VI's renunciation the tiara carries a very deep meaning that has not been stressed enough. Contrary to what I read some weeks ago, the Roman Curia is not the "the pope's court." The Church of God is governed by a college of bishops, in communion but scattered around the world, in whose service is the Bishop of Rome, whose Curia assists in this service. The "power"—this word the media loves so much to use—is not in the center; it is in the college as such, in light of the prerogatives linked to the function of him whom the Spirit places at the center of the brotherhood of bishops.

The theologians, a source of restlessness?

In the Church of God, among the numerous functions called forth by the Spirit, there is that of the theologians. Thomas Aquinas loved to speak of two chairs: that of the bishop and that of the theologian, *cathedra episcopi* and *cathedra magistri*. The function of the theologian is not easy or totally restful, especially during periods of great cultural change such as ours and when the theologian must give an opinion to bishops debating a difficult problem. Theologians know that their words can have a significant impact on the pastoral function. When theologians wish to be faithful servants of the Church under the light of the Gospel, their task can create for them problems of conscience: what to say and how to say it? All the more so since the media lies in wait and a phrase, minor to their eyes, might "make the front page" of the newspapers tomorrow. For example, I might have affirmed that "the pope must submit to the patriarch of Constantinople" when in fact I was commenting on a wonderful page of the *Tomos Agapis* of Paul VI and Athenagoras.

Theology is necessary for the Church. It must discover and understand, on the basis of the most painstaking research into Scripture and tradition, the genuine content and genuine meaning of revelation, discern what the apostolic community truly said about the moral imperatives of the Christian life. Belief in Christ is not the equivalent of a leap into the absurd. I am a Dominican. For the Thomist tradition, intelligence (reason and intuition) and the conscience retain their inalienable rights, in accord precisely with creation "in the image and likeness of God." A wise and intelligent God, revealed in his incarnate Logos, cannot tie the salvation of "his adopted children" to an abasement of intelligence and a slumbering of conscience. A healthy theology is a theology with a squint, because it has one eye fixed on the revealed given and the other eye fixed on the discoveries of intelligence, with the distance introduced there by philosophy. It is not simply a commentary on official texts, but it does its best to read them with these two eyes, the eye of the given, the eye of intelligence, enlightened by faith. Biblical theology, dogmatic theology, pastoral theology must state the same truth.

Faith is constantly a beggar of intelligence, and this is why, without the *cathedra magistri,* the *cathedra episcopi* quickly risks no longer being integrally faithful to the truth. In our time, the problems are numerous and complex where it is difficult to see clearly. I alluded to the perplexity of pastors confronted with discussions about the "Jesus of history and the Christ of faith." Still more tangled are moral questions, especially where the great human mystery of sexuality is at stake. The Church does not have to be enslaved by theories and ideas born in society, invading the media and dictating the law. It has to distance itself from them, especially when it suspects that these theories and ideas are not in harmony with God's will for humanity. Such a distancing belongs to its prophetic function. Often it is noted afterwards that the Church's resistance to certain currents was sound. Nevertheless, it is clear that all that disturbs the old ways of seeing is not blameworthy. It is necessary to study seriously the result of rigorous research, even if it is troubling. Here theology enters the scene. It enlightens the judgment to be rendered, but it often does this by trail and error. To be serious, it must be patient.

In his speech on October 9, 1999, at the Synod of Europe, Cardinal Martini spoke of certain "knots" of discipline and doctrine "which appear periodically as flash points on the Churches' way." He counted among these sexuality, the situation of women, the discipline of marriage; but also, on another level, the solution of the pastoral tragedy caused by the reduction in the number of ministers, the participation of the laity in some ministerial responsibilities, the practice of penitence, the relation between democracy and values, and the connection between moral law and civil legislation. These are all themes that theologians carefully study, for they know that they are for many Christians a source of anguish, leading on occasion to the abandonment of religious practice. Locally, bishops encourage theologians to continue their research and take up these problems. Bishops ask them specific questions: "What should be thought about the Orthodox position on remarriage, about which the Council of Trent wished to be discreet?"; "What should be thought about presbyterial ordination *de viri probati* [of experienced men] as in the East?" Theologians are aware, however, that this research irritates certain Roman circles, and that it is preferred that they remain quiet and provide commentary on present discipline rather than deepening the tradition to discover there new ways. "It is theologians who confuse everything," an ordinarily open and sympathetic "Roman" wrote to me after having read the article of an ethicist on divorce. I answered him with these two lines: "What would the Second Vatican Council have been like, which you said was a grace of God, without the support of the theologians?"

A new council?

Picking up an idea circulating for some years in several contexts, Cardinal Martini, in the same speech, evoked "the usefulness and almost the necessity of a collegial and authoritative consultation among all the bishops on certain crucial subjects which have appeared in the course of these forty years." His dream was the renewal of "the experience of communion, of the collegiality of the Holy Spirit" present at Vatican II. He specified later, however, that such an assembly could not be a council in the usual meaning of the word.

My judgment on this proposition is very nuanced. I cannot doubt the necessity of consultation among all the bishops on questions of doctrine and discipline that trouble the Church of God today. The obvious tensions between the Roman See and the local churches and, among various groups within them give rise to the fear of divisions in the Catholic Church. I am particularly struck by what I call the phenomenon of *estrangement.* This English term, difficult to translate into French, indicates the process by which human groups slowly come to feel themselves strangers to each other and to live as such. This happened to the Eastern and Western Churches, leading to a schism that still endures. Certain speeches at the regional synods convened by Rome give the impression that between the continents or subcontinents and Rome a separation or distancing, a cooling, has taken place. The same observation is valid within certain regions. It would be tragic if Rome were to speak with no one listening, as into a void. How would she then bind together the local churches, and how would they receive what, in God's design, they must receive from the ministry of the Bishop of Rome? In several places the present climate is not healthy. Underground schisms are even mentioned. A meeting of the type the cardinal of Milan proposes to resolve this situation would be of benefit to the faith both in the local churches and in Rome by reaffirming communion.

It appears to me, however, difficult to make the assembly a general council in the strict sense of the word, for two reasons especially. First, because the Second Vatican Council has not yet been completely "received." Present events show that on significant points the council's intentions are still only beginning to be implemented and have not yet fully penetrated attitudes. The reflections of the proposed assembly, which are so necessary, must be grounded on these intentions. Time to mature is still needed. It would be tragic if a too hasty discussion were to call into question fundamental achievements whose "reception" has not occurred. I am thinking, for example, of chapter 8 of *Lumen gentium* on Mary, which the bishops wanted "to prolong by a greater affirmation of mediation" *(sic).* This has weighty implications. Further, in the present ecumenical climate a general council seems to me to be unthinkable without an invitation to other Churches, particularly to the Eastern Churches, whose episcopate is recognized. Trent did it—with the mission to Ivan the Terrible entrusted to Canobio, with the dispatching of the Dominican Jules Staurianus to the Armenian patriarch—and in 1868 Pius IX had addressed the letter *Arcano divinae providentiae* to the Orthodox bishops. In both cases without success. Forgotten is John XXIII's speech to the priests of Rome, not published by *L'Osservatore romano,* where he affirmed his desire to put an end to the schism with Constantinople: "We will not hold an historical trial; we will not seek to see who was right and who was wrong. The responsibility is shared. We will only say: Let us reunite, let us end it with discussions." How would such an invitation be received today? It is impossible to say, in spite of John Paul II's continuing and courageous steps manifesting an unquestionable communion with the East. Refused, it would cause an ecumenical commotion. Accepted, it would necessitate changing the order of the day. It seems to me that it will be necessary to imagine a synod—rethought in its structure and its function—of the type of the extraordinary Synod of 1985, in conjunction with very particular gatherings of episcopal conferences.

Do you favor calling into question the necessity of the papacy?

No! Absolutely no. The papacy belongs to God's design for his Church. This cannot be called into question. I have always been very explicit on this point. In my speeches to the World Council and to Faith and Order I have constantly affirmed that the Catholic Church cannot renounce this ministry. Firmly situated within the vision of collegiality brought back to light by *Lumen gentium,* the papacy with its specificity belongs to the fiber of the Church of God. I have been shocked to read from the pen of a Catholic theologian that it is "an unavoidable evil." No! It is a good. For this reason, the document from ARCIC has rightly reconnected it to the gift of authority.

It has been said that to refuse to question this office, as you do, is a lack of intellectual and ecumenical courage.

Such an opinion scarcely makes sense. Certainly there are in the papacy some points that need reform. For a long time I have called attention to them. But this reform is precisely for the sake of permitting the papacy to be fully that which God wishes it to be. To wish to eliminate the papacy is not an attitude of courage. This is rather an abdication before others.

Would the East be able to assist the Catholic Church to discover an equilibrium between primacy and collegiality?

The East itself is divided. There is first of all the great split between the Churches that do and do not accept the Council of Chalcedon, the old dogmatic quarrel in which the two groups have exhausted themselves. There is next the climate of a tension created by the autocephalous Churches and nationalism, especially among the Churches in communion with Constantinople. The old temptation of phyletism, that is to say, of the identification of a Church and an ethnic group, condemned in 1872, is not fully overcome. In countries of emigration, referred to as the diaspora, several Orthodox Churches coexist, sometimes with less than warm relations. The "Holy and Great Council of the Orthodox Church," which, under the direction of Metropolitan Damaskinos, the Secretariat of Chambésy-Geneva, has undergone a long and careful preparation, is postponed from year to year. An Orthodox friend has whispered to me, humorously playing on an aggressive phrase from the encyclical of the patriarchs which in 1848 replied to Pius IX: "We would need to be infested by the papist heresy . . . and its centralizing venom." The East needs us quite as much as we need them.

The East is able to remind us, however, of a deep conviction, expressed in a very old document, Apostolic Canon 34, probably dating from 381:

> The bishops of every country ought to know who is the chief among them, and to esteem him as their head, and not to do any great thing without his consent; but every one to manage only the affairs that belong

to his own parish, and the places subject to it. But let him not do anything without the consent of all; for it is by this means there will be unanimity, and God will be glorified by Christ, in the Holy Spirit.

The international Catholic-Orthodox dialogue commission, begun in 1979, intended to study this text and to see how it applies not only to each nation but also to the *catholica* as such. Discussions on uniatism, however, have until now prevented this.

The East can help us also in its practice of synodal life. It varies by Church. The wish to include the entire community in major decisions concerning it, however, is clear in many of these Churches. Very hierarchical and very respectful of bishops (sometimes to an extreme for Western minds), they nevertheless know how to involve the laity. In Cyprus the laity take part in the election of the bishop and archbishop; at Alexandria they are included in the election of the patriarch. Ordinarily, theologians are laity, and they know themselves to be listened to and followed.

When you say that we are members of the last Catholic generations which lack humility, are you thinking about this need to "receive" from other Churches?

Yes, that is one of the aspects about which I am thinking, although it is not the only one. Let us speak first of the ecumenical "need." I say that we lack humility because we Catholics have the impression that we have much to give to other Christians and little to receive from them. Very often when we think of the other Churches—except perhaps the Orthodox Churches that ordinarily rank very high in our esteem—we have the tendency to regard them not only as different (which is true), but as inferior. We first fix our attention on whatever they lack. Ecumenical experience quickly teaches that they very often are able to realize and live out the Christian faith in a way that calls out to us. They do not have the papacy. They perhaps do not have the fullness of the means of salvation. They rarely possess the monastic life. They have little structure. However, their attachment to Christ and his Word can be fervent, their charity towards the most impoverished can be admirable. I thought of this when I saw members of the Salvation Army—a Christian organization although "nonliturgical," connected to the foundation of the World Council of Churches—take collections for immigrants in an almost Siberian cold.

Certainly, *Lumen gentium* assures us that the Catholic Church possesses the fullness of the means of salvation. Nevertheless, the Decree on

Ecumenism does not hesitate to affirm that elsewhere several of those means of salvation exist and they are "of great value." Moreover, it adds that it is not necessary to be silent about what the Spirit thus accomplishes in other communities, for this can contribute to the edification of Catholics, permit them to penetrate more fully into the mystery of Christ and of the Church. It is impossible, if we have understood that, to regard ourselves as the best. The record of grace is the reason for the institution's existence! Even in what concerns the institution itself, moreover, we have to learn from others. The Anglican Church, for example, can show us how better to connect episcopal ministry and synodality. The theologians and bishops of the Second Vatican Council received much from the non-Catholic observers, whose mark can be discerned in several texts. In launching the Catholic Church on the path of ecumenism, John XXIII and Paul VI have placed it on a road of humility.

But we have equally entered into another form of humility. Even after Vatican II, it was nearly impossible for a bishop or a Catholic theologian to affirm that in the past the Catholic Church had been wrong, that some popes had made bad decisions. It was always necessary to justify the past. Oh, the pirouettes made to show that the Declaration on Religious Liberty did not contradict the declarations of certain popes! Because I dared to criticize the *Dictatus Papae* of Gregory VII (while taking care to note that one must not "blacken his face too much"!), I myself have been called an "iconoclast"; I have been harshly reminded "that between a pope, even dead, and a theologian remains a wall of respect." Since Paul VI's short statement asking pardon from other Christians, this attitude has begun to change. John Paul II has prompted in the Catholic Church a vast movement of lucidity about the past and the truth. He encourages a *mea culpa* about the errors and the faults of its history. Old trials are reviewed. A new view of events results from taking history seriously. The truth is approached head on.

This turn has significant ecclesiological implications. It is not simply a question of making excuses. It is also necessary to engrave on the memory the shame of the accusation. The errors are not abolished by the simple act of confession. They remain with their consequences. The past is not able to be cleared away even if pardon is asked. In his letter on the preparation of the Jubilee in 2000, the Pope uses very strong expressions. The Catholic Church, he says, takes responsibility for the sin of its children, whose forms of thought and action have been veritable forms of counterwitness and of scandal. Among its errors he includes offenses against the unity of God's people; consent given to methods of intolerance and even of violence in the service of truth; responsibilities in the evils of our times; implication in serious forms of injustice and social marginalization; consent to the violation of human rights; and a too sluggish "reception" of Vatican II. He writes that to recognize these faults is a matter of loyalty and courage. As the history of these faults is disclosed, as Catholics recognize and repent of them, what Vladimir Jankelevitich has so well shown must be remembered: the *fecisse* (the thing done) is irretrievable. It is impossible to annihilate it: "What has been done cannot be undone." Clearly, in decades to come historians will pass probably severe judgments on our times. In spite of all our good intentions we ourselves are also fallible.

All this plunges us into a form of humility to which the Catholic Church officially has scarcely been accustomed. We are no longer able to present ourselves before other Christians and unbelievers as those who always have walked the straight and narrow, witnesses of a flawless faithfulness. In various periods of history, we have ourselves also participated in errors, often in atrocities. Sometimes even—as in the excesses of the Inquisition—we have developed particular practices hardly in harmony with the deep spirit of the Gospel. Theologians, bishops, popes have been implicated in situations or decisions that today are condemned. When in *Veritatis splendor* (no. 100) John Paul II strongly condemns slavery, he knows very well that his predecessors were silent until Paul III (in 1537) and, definitively, Gregory XVI (in 1839). When in *Evangelium vitae* (no. 56) he is severe toward the death penalty, he is not unaware that in 1184 Lucius III approved it for heretics . . .

A third reason today plunges us into total humility. We are no longer, as Christians, the strongly expanding religious group, imposing its law on societies, dominating culture. In our lands, the number of baptized and of those practicing Christianity are diminishing while Islam advances and the ancient religions attract followers. More than about humility, we should talk here about poverty . . .

Is this why you say that we are probably the last witnesses of a certain way of being Catholic?

Not entirely. I am thinking about the contrast between the Catholic Church in the West and the Catholic Church on other continents. As is normal, we live presently in a Catholicism that was shaped and developed for millennia in a West with very characteristic cultural values. The break between the Christian East has further accented the more and more Latin features, which have, as it were, passed into the flesh of the Catholic Church, causing the disappearance of such rich cultural features as those of the Celts. Missionaries transplanted this Latin Catholicism to the regions they evangelized. I recall from my youth missionaries happy to show how they had reproduced in their mission village the church of their home parish and had given it as a patron the name of this parish. To encourage our choir, they told us that young Africans sang better than we the Latin chants. In brief, the Catholic Church was Latin.

I constantly warn my Orthodox students against too quickly criticizing this Latin Church that they reproach for giving birth to Christendom. Latin patristics has an extreme richness. The Latin liturgy has great beauty if for no other reason than Gregorian chant and the style of its hymns. Romanesque and Gothic architecture, as also certain Baroque monuments, are splendid. The culture transmitted in the schools and universities of the West has a rare quality. Moreover, it is especially the Latin Church that has preached the Gospel as far as the most distant lands.

We have said that in the West there is a crisis in the Church. Its word seems ignored, relegated to the sphere of the private. Its ministers decline. Even in countries such as France and England, Islam threatens to surpass it in numbers. It attracts few, and the young are more and more scarce at Sunday Mass. Christianity now slowly moves from this West, where it suffers so, toward other continents with all that this passage implies. The regional synods of recent years have shown how deep is the desire for a true inculturation of the faith. It must not lead to new truths—this would be a betrayal of revelation—but to new expressions of revelation, to new balances. Today Asians, Africans, Polynesians are not comfortable with the doctrinal elaboration where Greek concepts hold a critical place (the "consubstantial" of the Creed, the idea of hypostatic union, the definition of person). Tomorrow, probably Westerners will in turn be uncomfortable with an expression of faith relying on other modes of thought. Already this is the experience in certain meetings of the World Council of Churches. The Church's center of influence is shifting and the change will not only be geographic. The Western view will no longer necessarily impose itself and set the norm for all ranges of ecclesial life. For example, when Faith and Order prepared its explanation of the faith of Nicaea-Constantinople, several persons asked that the term "consubstantial"—which was at the heart of the conciliar debates—be kept (in parentheses) as an expression of the traditional faith, but that it no longer be made "the only normative term." An equivalent is to be found for each cultural group. Would you like a simpler example of this shift of which I am speaking? In the past Canada has been one of the great missionary countries, establishing several Churches abroad. Today, because of the increasing scarcity of vocations for ministry, there are African priests who are pastors in several parishes of two dioceses which I know the best, Ottawa and Gatineau. Now parishes note a change in the manner of celebration, of preaching, of marital counseling. "They are our missionaries, and our diocese takes on the color of a small Africa," one of these parishioners told me with a little humor.

It is not only at this level that "we are the last witnesses of a way of living out Christianity." The reduction in the number of "practicing" Catholics and even of the baptized leads in the majority of Western countries to stunning changes in the structure of local churches. Parishes are reorganized and some are suppressed. Some private, prestigious institutions (schools, colleges, and hospitals) are closed. New forms of councils are created; laity are entrusted with highly significant responsibilities. The classical religious communities recede. The Sunday Eucharist is no longer weekly and is replaced by a Liturgy of the Word. Other modifications could be mentioned that are less obvious. Soon there will probably be a reorganization of neighboring dioceses. The Church will be declericalized, but this process has many consequences for the way the faith is lived in the community. The image of the parish grouped around the priest, who was always available, aware of all the sorrows and joys, is disappearing. In certain corners I know, this runs the risk of depopulating churches even more, if one is not able to react in time.

There are still other causes of change in the West. In order that the young generations feel at ease, certain forms of their social conduct, certain surprising aspects of their morals are accepted. High-school chaplaincies no longer have the "wisdom" of earlier times. I'll always remember the terrified cry of a friend's spouse, a former instructor, seeing at a Eucharist in preparation for world youth day the archbishop enter with a green-haired punk as acolyte, a ring in his nose and another in his left ear, not to speak of multicolored shorts, while guitars played music that scarcely resembled Bach or Handel. Without a doubt this is excessive. But I told this friend what consoles me personally when faced with initiatives which appear to me to be strange. At our Eucharists, some youths yawn and are bored. They do not open their mouths when one starts to sing Deiss or classical chant is begun. Now it's our turn to accept having our ears irritated by a new music, our eyes shocked by an esthetic with a taste surprising for us, but with the hope that an authentic faith is expressed there and that good taste will triumph. In the face of to-morrow's Church, we would probably be as surprised as our grand-parents were in the face of the Church of Vatican II with its altars facing the people, its Masses without Latin, its priests without cassocks, its Sovereign Pontiff traveling around the world, its kisses of peace be-tween Catholics and "schismatics." . . . The Church is in historical flux.

Would the "sin against the Spirit" of today's Church be to reject this evolution?

It is difficult to speak of a "sin against the Spirit" because no one truly knows what is in question. Without a doubt in Mark (3:29) it is a refusal to be guided by the Spirit and to attribute to God what comes from God, seeing there rather the mark of the Evil One. We can say that if the Church refused to evolve, to read "the signs of the times," it would refuse the Spirit. But it is always imprudent to label such and such a fact, such and such a behavior as a sin against the Spirit. I would not dare say, for example, that the abuse of norms and prescriptions, often suffocating, is a sin against the Spirit. I see there rather, especially when those who decree them do not know the concrete, sometimes tragic, situations where they must be applied, a lack of wisdom or pru-dence. What is needed is a greater integration of those interested, when they are competent, in the elaboration of texts, normative or otherwise, which concern them.

On the other hand, I would be less hesitant to label as "sin against the Spirit" the refusal to work for the disappearance of the scandal of the division of Christians. I have said that since John XXIII, but espe-cially thanks to Paul VI and John Paul II, the Catholic Church has en-tered with clarity and courage into the field of ecumenical work. However, one must clearly note that while the Bishop of Rome contin-ues to advocate steps toward unity, while the Pontifical Council for Christian Unity endeavors to put flesh on the dialogues with other Christians, the people of God have lost their enthusiasm. Involved in the ecumenical task since the Uppsala Assembly of the World Council of Churches (1968) and having responsibilities in Faith and Order, I am able to gage this cooling off of ardor in the quest for communion. It is a matter for the experts. On the ground one finds two attitudes. A lax-ist attitude forgets the demands of true ecumenism. Intercommunion is expanded; ecumenism is transformed into indifferentism; "all religions have value." In opposition, a rigorist attitude no longer cares to estab-lish connections, to know and mutually assist others. Ecumenism comes to be ignored. Both attitudes evince a deep scorn for the unity God wishes; eyes are closed to the appeal of the Gospel. Twenty years ago the announcement of a conference focusing on unity filled the room; today it attracts a few people with gray hair. Ten years ago the Week of Prayer for Christian Unity was a great moment in the life of the diocese; today you find yourself among "old militants, saddened to see so few young heads," notes a national leader. The Lutheran-Catholic declaration has caused a certain jolt in several places. Will it last? Because of an obvious slowness, especially on the Catholic side, in welcoming of the results of dialogue, there is a weariness. Interest is lost. A spare-time activity of theologians, one says. An Anglican friend remarks: "The Vatican intensely pushes the dialogue but seems to fear welcoming its fruits . . . Would this be because it fears them?"

I said that I would, with caution, label as "sin against the Spirit" the refusal to hear the ecumenical call because the future of the Gospel is at stake. These men and women who present themselves before the world as disciples of Christ the Reconciler, members of his Body of reconciliation and communion, carriers of his Spirit, the Spirit of reconciliation and communion, are internally split and incapable of being reconciled one with another. If it were only a question of trite quarrels, it would not be tragic. But the tragedy is that they are divided even in their understanding of the essential elements of revelation and the celebration of the sacraments. In this situation, the Churches destroy the credibility of the Gospel of God. Even more, they proclaim in fact that the power of division—one of the main faces of the power of evil—prevails over that of the Cross. Even these men and women, who explicitly affirm having received at baptism the Spirit of Christ "putting to death hostility," are in conflict on essentials. Without exception, things being what they are, the Churches contradict by their division what they confess in their baptism. Thus they render the Gospel unacceptable to many men and women who desperately seek salvation. Their division is an offense against God and his design; this is why it becomes an offense against their brothers and sisters who seek God. So I say that to refuse the ecumenical call today is a matter of the deepest gravity.

To what kind of Christianity would the Churches in communion be witnesses?

I have spoken of reconciliation and will not take it up again. I would insist especially on one point that receives very little stress. It is clear that nations and societies are no longer officially Christian and that they no longer identify their values with those of Christianity, even in the United States where candidates for election quote the Gospel . . . This has consequences for mission. The Churches can no longer attempt to cling to the powers that be. They can rely only on the power of their own witness to Christ. I love to say that they have to be Christian without respect for persons. I thus translate a Greek term, *parresia*, which the New Testament uses. Among its numerous meanings is that of "self-confidence," "daring," "proud freedom." The apostolic texts are all marked by this pride of belonging to Christ and of living the Gospel *at all costs*. Without sinking into proselytism or a propaganda of bad taste beloved by some groups with their posters or their enticing stickers, Christians should not be ashamed of calling on the Spirit of Christ. This requires, obviously, that they not be in contradiction with the will of Christ as they are in their confessional divisions. When the Churches, speaking with one voice with secular movements, talk of peace, of defense of personal rights, of justice, of the respect for human dignity, they must not fear to confess that they find their inspiration in the Gospel. All the more so—although it would be neither wise nor prudent to boast about it—since many of these movements are Christian in their origin. A necessary discretion is confused with a total silence about Christ on the pretext of needing to appear neutral before a society that proclaims itself religiously neutral. This has always irritated me, especially when those who talk this way are ministers, clearly identified as such. One cannot renounce what one is.

At its meeting in Bangalore (in 1978), the Commission on Faith and Order had already launched a study on martyrdom. With panache, Annie Jaubert, since deceased, showed there how *parresia* before the world's powers is the urgent duty of the Churches. Faced with this duty, they cannot compromise. They need, however, to find the most fitting way to accomplish this without falling into fanaticism and without transforming their action into a counterwitness by advocating repugnant methods of protesting practices they reject. Clear vision is not always easy here. In communion, pooling their experience, the reconciled Churches could here be one. They are called to a common witness to the person willed by God, to the humanity willed by God.

What is this humanity willed by God? Some episcopal conferences, like the one in France, some heads of Churches, like John Paul II and the archbishop of Canterbury, George Carey, often examine its features. Certainly, several of the features are encountered in our societies that are not some monsters of inhumanity and bear the mark of God the

Creator. There is found generosity, the love of liberty, the quest for justice, and many other things. But these values are realized in a profound disarray, stemming from the power of other forces such as the consent to the tyranny of money, insidious violence exercised by the media, the slavery of sex.

Here especially is manifest the "Gospel difference." It is revealed in the life of Jesus Christ and his Sermon on the Mount, but the apostolic letters already permit a closer definition. Its principal characteristics are well known: the radicality of the gift of self; the priority of the love of others over the quest of one's personal dreams; the gratuitousness of acts, even giving one's coat to the person who asks only for the shirt; refusal of revenge reaching even to offering one's left cheek to the person who has slapped the right; pardon without limit; attention to those who are crushed by suffering or scorn. These are some of the practices not usually found in our societies. I am anxious to add here two features often forgotten, no doubt because their roots are more evident in the Old Testament. They seem to me more and more essential in our world. First, the refusal of all idols, the old idols that never disappeared but take new names; the new idols that our cultures cause to spring up in all areas. Finally, the absolute priority accorded to God. In a world where God is spoken of less and less, where (we are told) "a reason for the success of Buddhism in the West is that it is without God," Christians faithful to the Gospel stake everything on God, place the relation to the God and Father of Jesus Christ at the heart of their existence.

Whoever knows a bit about humanity understands how the encounter of Christian groups striving to incarnate this "Gospel difference" often provokes astonishment, heckling, a question, an affinity. We know the attraction exercised, even on unbelievers, by contemplative or monastic communities true to their ideal, while able to make it contemporary. They are so distant from the customs of the world; and that these who make this "difference" the law of their existence are happy and joyful surprises, men and women saturated with the ideas of the century, so that they wonder: What is this Jesus? What is this Gospel? But that is not only true of religious communities. I am thinking about Jacques and Raissa Maritain and about the letter from Jean Cocteau: "You have pushed me, pushed like a man who kills," pushed on the way that leads to God. I am thinking about Madeleine Delbrêl. Going back further in the past, I am thinking about Ozanam (who died in 1853) and his wife. The attractive power of God's Church does not lie in its condemnation of society but in the concrete presence in its midst of men

47

and women living with "a saved heart" and having the boldness (the *parresia*) to confess from where this salvation comes. The "Gospel difference" smashes to bits the walls of suspicion.

It has been written that the Church is dying, that we are the last Christians . . .

Against this opinion, which spreads thoughtlessly, I have written my little book, *Sommes-nous les derniers chrétiens?* [Are We the Last Christians?]. I recognize that the Church is wounded, and I share the deep anxiety of several bishops in the regional synods. Often I meditate on the troubling phrase of Luke, "When the Son of Man comes, will he discover faith on the earth?" (Luke 18:8) and that of Paul on apostasy and the power of distraction (2 Thess 2:3). The commentaries of the exegetes have until now scarcely explained this to me. But from instinct—the instinct of my *sensus fidei*—I say no to this opinion.

Why? First because I believe in God, the Creator and the Savior, the one of the *Credo*. Then because I compare the very nature of the Gospel with the desire which does not cease to dwell in the deepest part of the human heart.

I have spoken much up to now about the Gospel, and I do not wish to repeat myself. I wish simply to say that the Gospel is the Good News of a God who has created humanity for happiness and who in spite of sin has not changed his design. Thomas Aquinas understood this very well, and this is why he conceived Christian ethics as an ethic of happiness. Especially in Luke's Gospel, the ministry of Jesus is, as it were, tightly enclosed in this dynamism of happiness offered unhappy humanity. It opens with the great declaration in the synagogue: "The Spirit of God . . . has sent me to announce to the poor the Good News . . . liberation . . . recovery of sight . . . freedom . . . the year of the Lord's favor." It ends with the word to the thief: "You will be with me in paradise." The Son is sent to return humanity, suffering and unhappy, to the road of happiness. The Gospel is a message of hope and its instructions are nothing other than the merciful indication of the way to enter into the blessedness of the kingdom. Jesus reveals God's work only by taking on himself the tragic condition of an accursed person (Gal 3:13). Gripped by the darkness of the absurd, he cries on the cross to the Father: "Why have you forsaken me?" I have been impressed for a long time by this close connection between the Passion, where the Gospel reaches its summit, and Jesus in distress before his Father, no longer finding the meaning of his destiny and of his mission.

Here, the Gospel appears to me very close to men and women of our time. Our contemporaries, placed in an often cruel world from which every shred of humanity fades, are in quest of meaning. Particularly through novels that mirror society and the existence it imposes, literature reminds us how much they feel themselves disarmed, searching desperately for some value to cling to so they will not sink. The future is no longer clear. Is our world forever deserted by true happiness, inhabited by violence, led by the quest of profit? There had been a belief in the utopia of progress. Little clarity is now needed to realize that if in certain areas—travel, technology, especially health—life has become simpler, in the other areas life is still more somber. What will be the future? One can only be anxious before certain facts, such as what one newspaper considers "the most important feat of the last century, the cloned sheep, Dolly." Who says that this "new nature" is not the source of a new, unpredictable distress?

This harshness of life and concern for tomorrow give rise, for many, to a question: "Why am I here? What is the why, the meaning of my presence?" The cry of Job—"cursed be the day that saw my birth"—and that of Jeremiah—"cursed be the day when my mother gave me birth"—are today the cries of thousands of men and women of every age and every condition. I read in a scientific magazine this letter of a twenty-two-year-old young woman to her parents: "I can no longer endure my existence. You who have caused my birth, assist me to leave it; my life no longer has any meaning; if you truly love me, do it." This distress is too common and the decisions to which it leads are too irreparable for us to consider the question of the meaning of existence as secondary. Rare are those who, when great hardships suddenly appear, do not seek their reason for being. Antoine de Saint-Exupéry suggested that the quest for meaning is as urgent as the search for the smallest drop of water by a person going in circles in the desert. Specialists thus explain the success of gurus, magi, sects, and the destructive disillusions of some of their followers.

How would God the Creator, who sent his well-beloved Son into just this tragedy of humanity's distress, even to the dramatic question which escapes from his lips on the cross, be able to abandon humanity in the middle of such a crisis of hope? How in the faces and in the words of pain of these men and women would God not recognize the tears of his Son and not hear his *Eli, Eli lema sabaqthani*? In his faithfulness, God cannot allow the light to die which in the one crucified and resurrected he lit in the midst of the darkness (of hatred, of envy, of pride) that unceasingly obscures the destiny of humanity. I dare to say that if he did so, God the Father would have called into question the eternal love that ties him to the Son; he would not respect the greatness of the Son's obedience: "I have finished the work which you have given me to do." God owes it to his Son. I even think that this belongs to his glorification about which the seventeenth chapter of John's Gospel speaks. This Gospel must always resound in humanity.

This last sentence can surprise. But it is the meaning of one aspect of the Church, little highlighted in the Catholic tradition, its inde-fectibility. During the last centuries, infallibility has so dominated our attention that we have neglected to examine why it exists and what is the point of Christ's answer to Peter's confession. To reduce inde-fectibility to a matter of the presence or absence of sin in the Church, as several Lutherans and Reformed do, appears to me inadequate. It is es-sentially a question of indestructibility, permanence, maintenance, con-tinuity. The forces of evil can try to destroy the Church and perhaps to sow in it some ferment of death. In spite of everything, the Church will fulfill its mission of salvation. Not because of its own merits, but be-cause of God's faithfulness. On the day of the Parousia of the Lord, the Church will still be there because the love of God for humanity will not be extinguished. In what condition will the Church be? God alone knows. But—perhaps reduced to a "remnant"—the Gospel will have continued to be proclaimed by it, and the means of salvation will not have ceased to be offered. The agent responsible for this *perpetuitas* is obviously the Spirit whose action always has an eschatological color, that is to say, as the Orthodox tradition teaches, that it has already caused the appearance of "what will be at the end of all." Because God cannot take back his Spirit, he cannot allow the source of faith and grace in his Church to run dry. It might be that the Church, like the apostles' small boat, is tossed on every side by the storm, that its sail rips, even that the waves overwhelm it. Today we are experiencing that. It might also be that in some regions it is destroyed, as was the case in North Africa, as I mentioned. We fear such today in certain countries. Perhaps the Church will be as poor as Christ in his Passion. But the Spirit will not leave it, and God will not reconstitute it into something else.

Must I here only repeat pious formulae rightly to carry out my task as a Catholic theologian and to justify my ecumenical work? A former student, who became an agnostic, often repeats to me: "The Church is in agony, it is useless to exhaust yourself putting the pieces that remain in the same basket." Well, no. What I have just stated responds to a deep conviction. I do not like to speak of my intimate feelings, and those who live with me know this well. Nothing angers me more than the striptease of those who lay their hearts bare on the least occasion. This is the source of my allergy to certain forms of the charismatic movement. I equally flee talkative men and women, getting us drunk on the account of their feats. I can at least repeat what I have already written. My Dominican life allows great spaces of contemplation and silence. These are the moments when the memory of wounds, deceptions, maulings, jealousies (the great ecclesiastical evil), concerns for the future settle out and the consciousness of God's grace is deepened. Then spring to mind several verses of psalms that the monastic liturgy has me sing daily, Gospel stories, Johannine literature, letters of the apostles, in particular the letter to the Ephesians. This sheaf of verses which populates my believing memory is bound by the words that John's Gospel places on Peter's lips: "To whom will we go, Lord Jesus?" The question is without nuances. For two millennia, going straightaway to this confession which concludes the chapter on the Bread of Life, men and women of absolute poverty have reread it in the light of their experience and their desire. They hold it as true, capable of infusing meaning into their existence. I am one of them. Peter gives as the reason for his radical attachment to Christ Jesus: "You have the words of eternal life." It is a matter of far more than words announced explicitly by Jesus, but of all that his mystery implies, his *acta et dicta*. An old Anglican exegete, B. F. Westcott, whom I often consult, comments thus: "The Apostles found in Jesus Christ all that they could seek" in the necessities and the deep desire of their existence. It seems to me that no one has said it better to our time than François Mauriac in a few lines of his *Nouveaux memoires intérierurs*. I encounter there, expressed in a splendid style, what is at the heart of my own response to the "to whom shall we go?":

> Creatures are loved as they are, in spite of what they are, because of what they strive to be and what they long to be . . . [God] keeps in his sight . . . poor hearts gathered from all the countries of the earth, purified of their blemishes and who address him by the names which the Church breathes . . . Father of the poor, Light of hearts, supreme Comforter, Rest in our labors, Peace in our passions, Comfort for our tears (*Nouveaux memoires intérieurs*, Paris, pp. 149–50).

Christ Jesus is the incarnation of the Good News of mercy, of the pardon which forbids withdrawing into guilt and opens onto the future, of the hope of communion, of the existence that finds its meaning in the gift of oneself, of the God who gives himself. I frequently wonder what I would become if this reference to Christ was torn from my life. I would probably be like a ship on a starless night, having lost its compass.

This is not simply a personal affair. Let's open the books of Christians such as Augustine, Chrysostom, Pascal, Mauriac. The answer of poor Peter quickly appears like the main theme of their destiny as baptized persons, those also torn by life, tormented. They are what they are because of Jesus Christ whose Good News they have internalized by making it the inspiration of their existence. The serious theologian knows that such an option cannot rashly be rejected as an illusion. To my students, sometimes tempted to start everything again at zero, I quote a wise remark of Samuel Taylor Coleridge found in the work of John Stuart Mill: "What was held as truth by sensible people throughout long generations cannot be rejected out of hand as pure and simple error, but it ought to respond at least to an important part of reality." My poor experience joins this line of men and women who are worth a thousand times more than I. Gathering together what I know of the human condition (from myself or others) and what my faith teaches of the God and the Father of the Lord Jesus Christ, I say like those before me that Peter's question is not pure rhetoric, that it is rooted in reality. I say this in church, knowing that the Holy Spirit says it in me and that the Spirit confirms it by the witness of other Christians in the mysterious solidarity of the "communion of the saints."

That is why I affirm that as long as there will be men and women seeking the meaning of their existence and others speaking to them the name of Christ, knowing what it means, there will be Christians. Picking up again the last lines of *Ce que je crois* from this fiery Christian, Maurice Clavel, I may add that they will only know how to proclaim their *Credo* "by pronouncing it with other men," and thus in church.

Even more, I repeat—because this appears to me more and more significant—that, like this same Clavel thinking of the influence of Mauriac on him, each will confess: "Christ has called me by my name through persons who knew his name" (p. 293). Clavel here makes his own the witness of a young convert "like any other," read in a magazine. In my research on *koinonia (communion)*, I have been struck by this observation: at the beginning of faith there is normally the *communion* of a restlessness and of a witnessing. *Communion* is thus at the start, at the center, and at the end of the life in Jesus Christ. This is why the Church is *communion*. A communion which takes seriously human questions. A *communion* which comes from afar.

According to you, this Church has roots which go deep into history . . .

This question would require a long response. The present research on the Jesus of history and the Christ of faith highlights the Jewishness of Jesus and the planting of his work in the soil of Judaism. Jesus cannot be torn from his context. I read with great interest the works of a scholar such as E. P. Sanders who insists on the connection between the vocation of Jesus and the great desire for the gathering of Israel for God's supreme "visitation." Theologian that I am, I think that the Christian novelty—what I called in responding to another question "the Gospel difference"—is set within this milieu. How to understand the Eucharist itself without reference to Jewish literature? The Church of God is "the fulfillment" of the hope of Israel, but in an until then undreamt extension. The universalist intuitions penetrating certain pages of prophetic literature become, especially in the Acts of the Apostles and Paul, essential features of the Church. It is the Church of God. When Jesus states that he has come only to the lost sheep of Israel, to whom he first sends his disciples, he is operating within Jewish logic. However, when the evangelists—before the mission given to their readers to proclaim the Gospel throughout the entire world (Mark 16:15; Matt 28:19; Luke 24:47)—take care to note Jesus' concessions to a ministry beyond the Jewish limits (the Syro-Phoenician woman, the Gerasene demoniac, the deaf-mute of the Decapolis, the second multiplication of the bread . . .) they reconnect with the universalist opening of second Isaiah, with Jeremiah 16, with Zechariah, with Jonah and Psalm 87. Christ Jesus is unintelligible without his roots among his people; the New Testament without its articulation of the Old; the Christian faith without the faith of Israel; the novelty of the Gospel without its soil as old as that of the holy people; the Church of Pentecost without the people of Sinai. The community of Pentecost is just beneath the surface of the assembly of the desert. The Cross and the Resurrection cause it to emerge. Since the beginning of my studies at Saulchoir, I have studied this connection, this symphony, and it has become one of the fundamental inspirations of my teaching. I am often asked why I speak of the Church of God, *ekklesia tou Theou*. Here is the explanation.

The first schism, and the most weighted with consequences, is without any doubt the rupture between Israel and the Church, a rupture in the Church of God. Is it possible to have a Church cut from the whole Church of God, any more than it is possible to have a Gospel cut from the entire Gospel of God? The Christian Church lives from this instinct.

Its prayer is that of the psalms, its Scripture is the entire Bible. Its faith is that of Abraham, Isaac, and Jacob. It knows, to repeat with the liturgy the words of Peter under the portico of Solomon, that "the God of Abraham, Isaac and Jacob, the God of the Fathers is he who has glorified Jesus his servant." The Cross, just as the letter to the Ephesians understands it, smashes "the wall of separation" *(to mesotoichon tou phragmoi)*, which the *Letter of Aristeas* said placed the Jews "totally apart from humanity." A Scandinavian exegete thinks to find there even some recollection of Isaiah 5:5 (Thorston Moritz, *A Profound Mystery*, Leiden, 1996, pp. 40–42).

The roots of the Church of God go even more deeply into the soil of humanity. It is, as Augustine so well understood, *"jam ab Abel justo"* [since Abel the Just]: "The Church was not absent at the beginning of the human race" (*Enar. In Ps. 118*, 29.9). The theme will be repeated by Gregory the Great, the Middle Ages, even Luther. Prosper of Aquitaine, a contemporary of Augustine, does not hesitate to write that what the Law and the Prophets realized in Israel is already accomplished through other means for the gathering of the nations (*De vocatione omnium gentium,* II, 5). By chance, with an article in mind, I have the text at hand. Therefore I can quote it:

> Would anyone be able to doubt that all human beings, whatever their nation or their time, who have been able to please God, have been distinguished by the Spirit of divine grace? Certainly, in the past, this grace was more parsimonious and more hidden; nevertheless it has not been refused in any age, always the same in effectiveness but different in quantity, according to an unchangeable design but different modalities.

The thinking of Justin, with his *semina verbi*, is known. He affirms that, in paganism, people were mysteriously enlightened by the Word of God. I love to recall a phrase, it seems to me little known, of Leo the Great: "What the incarnation brings about concerned the past as much as the future; no age, however far back it may be, was deprived of the sacrament of human salvation" (*Sermo 3* On the Nativity, 4).

Theological research on ancient religions has indeed allowed us to perceive how the Word of God is at work in the great religious aspirations that maintain humanity in a state of spiritual wakefulness. When the letter to the Colossians speaks of the Son (and not of the Word), it sees there the one in whom, by whom, for whom everything has been created, the one who is "before all." It does not separate the Son from his Church. This point has impressed me for a long time. Against overly shortsighted ecclesiologies, which only examine the reality of the Church of God in a linear fashion, beginning with the New Testament, I have always held that the Church starts to germinate from the beginning, extending its roots *"jam ab Abel justo."* Its source is obviously the paschal mystery of Christ Jesus. The Cross is the temporal event of history from which it becomes visible and reveals its identity. But Thomas Aquinas has taught me that, since Christ is one with the eternal Word for whom all times are in one eternal moment, the power of the Cross was able to act "from before the Incarnation": the moment of the Cross is seized in the flash of eternity.

Does this further strengthen you in your conviction that the Church cannot perish and that we are not the last Christians?

Obviously. A faithfulness of God toward humanity, so radical and so inclusive, must last until the end of history. As I have said in the preceding answer, the Church of God is both the revelation and the realization of this tenderness of God embracing human destiny in the particularity of its joys but also (and perhaps especially) of its distresses. God does not wish humanity to be without hope, and humanity does not wish to be without hope. My conviction is found at the intersection of these two certainties, all the while knowing that it is God who places in the human heart the desire and the hope which are grafted there. Nicolas Berdyaev, at the zenith of Marxism, saw even there a messianic dream (Marx was a Jew) where this hope, badly served by Christianity, sought to find itself: a substitute for a humanity no longer able to contain its hope, an explosion of an unsatisfied excess, a burst of an unconscious need "of new heavens and a new earth" so urgent is this need, "a reminder of unfinished duty." Augustine said that God created humans "to be desirous" and that all his work is to satisfy this desire. The Church is born in the space of this desire at the beginning of hope. I do not know what, under the leadership of the Spirit, the Church is called to become in the coming centuries. But I believe in my faith that the Church will be there at the day of the Lord, a servant of the mercy-faithfulness *(hesed-we-emeth).*

For you, the Church and faith seem not to pose a problem, and yet to read you, we see a restless Christian. Can you clarify this apparent contradiction?

Yes, I am a restless Christian. I get it from my Dominican vocation. We are restless people, and if we must believe what old Father Bochenski

grumbled on the eve of his death, this restlessness often makes us unbearable "to the hierarchy eager for good disciples." But here it is indeed necessary to distinguish different levels. Faith is first, and at its
very root, total confidence in God who is "faithful." At this level, I am
not a restless person. But the faith—from the New Testament on—indicates also the collection of truths connected to this confidence, the manner in which the Churches offer them or understand them. Then I am
restless. A bundle of concerns focusing on particular points, not an over-
all restlessness. Does the West in the presentation of the truth of the
Gospel take sufficient account of all the complexity of humanity, of the
heart as much as of reason? Is there enough respect for the historicity of
humanity? Is there a total coherence with the great principles declared
to be fundamental? Does one understand how to capture and understand the *sensus fidelium*? Is full attention given to respecting conscience
on moral matters? Is there a conviction, as in the East (wiser than we are
in this area), of the absolute transcendence of the truth of the salvation
which God alone can "understand" and state "as it is"? Does one avoid
the temptation to weigh down uselessly the content of the "truths to be
believed" rather than concentrate on the essential? Is not the manner of
expression, especially on important subjects, too obsolete to be well
understood? Is there still the sense of analogy? One senses that my ecumenical work increases this restlessness. A poorly chosen word is
enough—as the mention of Anglican ordinations in the official commentary on *Ad tuendam fidem*—for all confidence to collapse and for one
to search for unavowed intentions. Each time an official document is
promulgated, all these questions come to my mind. The answer I give
to them brings me pain. The Church is steeped in poverty, and it is not
always the poverty I earlier praised.

*There is also the poverty that comes from what opposes the Church: atheism,
persecution . . .*

Since the Cross of Calvary, the Church has been prey to a savage
hatred of Christ. It has resisted. It has never disappeared. I see there the
sign of the mysterious covenant between it and the humanity of which
I speak. Throughout all history, there has been a wish to eliminate, to
wipe out, the memory of Christ. From the beginning his apostles are put
to death; communities that invoke him are persecuted; martyrs multi-
ply. This will continue and still continues in certain regions of Asia and
Africa. My ecumenical contacts with Orthodoxy allowed me, during the

atrocious time of the Iron Curtain, to discover the tricks of this resolute wish to tear from human existence any reference to Christ. The ferocity shown in this enterprise did not arise spontaneously. It had—with obviously less odiousness—some common root even with the gentler struggle of a Voltaire against "the infamy," a word designating less Christianity as such than fanaticism and the superstition which he believed the Church connected with Christ. Voltaire was a theist, not an atheist. By contrast, the atheism of a Comte, a Nietzsche, a Marx, and then of a Hitler, such atheism sought, in rejecting God and Christ, to impose a new finality on existence, erasing faith in God forever. Finished is the infancy of humanity! Finished is the grip "of an invention of the Jew," Hitler screamed. In spite of attempts and efforts aiming at destroying them, the memory of Christ remains, the Church abides, wounded but still standing. It is humanity that has thereby lost its liberty and been thrust into an abyss of evil from which it has not recovered. In their turn, our contemporaries begin to discover that their new idols also cannot destroy the memory of Christ. It unexpectedly reappears. It does not dissolve into modernity. New insights do not render it pointless. I have noted in a shrewd analyst of our societies, Jean Claude Guillebaud, a remark on these forms of renewal that offer everyone "the happiness of the day and the magnificence of the moment which passes": they impugn hope (*La refondation du monde*, Paris, 1999, p. 121). Whence their fragility.

In a famous phrase of his *Apology* Tertullian defined the blood of the martyrs as the seed of Christians. This has unfortunately been turned into a slogan. But I very often wonder how it happens that so many swords, beasts of the circus, fires, stakes, ropes, bullets, tortures, freezing jails, daggers, execution posts have not succeeded in causing the disappearance of the small handful of Jews, then the small handful of powerless disciples invoking a crucified man. If Christians have such resistance, is it not because God is there for something?

You use a beautiful image to express this hope, that of the polygonum. Can you explain this image?

The image of the polygonum has had some success. A compatriot told me how, during a flight, he was seated near two passengers who, on learning that he was from Saint Pierre-et-Miquelon, asked him about . . . the polygonum, to his surprise. He claims to have answered them: "It is an invader which I do not appreciate." I, on the contrary, having neither a garden nor a paved courtyard—I love it very much for its color, its elegance, its shrubbery, its ecological function, above all its symbolism. If a polygonum has grown somewhere, you will not be able to get rid of it: one fine day, to your surprise, it will timidly reappear, then spread. A little morsel of root hidden between two clumps of earth is enough for the whole plant to regain life. Why? First, certainly, because it is a hardy plant, resisting all injuries caused by weather and by human beings (who uproot it, mow it, spray it with strong weed-killers). But especially because there is between it and the soil a secret agreement that the mineral salts filling its roots purify and enrich. The earth of my island, stony, often scattered by violent winds, has made an alliance with the polygonum in order not to become a sterile rock. I find its despisers ungrateful in this regard.

The symbolism is clear. At the depths of desire, a covenant exists between humanity (also swept by hurricanes) and the Gospel. If you try to uproot the Gospel, one day it will spring up anew, in spite of your persecutions, your blood baths, or your ideological propaganda. For, by the call rooted by God in its desire, humanity will always refuse to be without hope.

As we finish, I would like to invoke two facts, one already old, the other very recent. First, the horrified astonishment of a Soviet Communist engineer, a zealous destroyer of the Orthodox faith, who had seen fall from the pocket of his more brilliant colleague a small icon of the Virgin of Vladimir, all covered with silver and shiny from wear. Then the story of a high-school teacher, a mediocre philosopher, endlessly making a laughingstock of a Christianity described as "bastion of religious obscurantism," making Jesus "a hero invented by a few hysterics" and to whom his students come to ask that someone be invited to speak to them about Christ. For, "after all that you have said, this individual interests us." Like the polygonum, Christ resists destruction. The slightest thing and he is reborn. In *The Idiot* (it seems to me) Dostoevsky speaks of is an elusive something that the reasonings of the atheists cannot define.

Let us return to your quotation of Yossel Rakover, "I will always believe in you, even despite you."

I have already explained myself. There are strange moments in life when, even though the impossible has been done for the service of the Gospel, all collapses. You have relentlessly prepared an important meeting and then illness arises preventing you from any participation. Even worse, you then receive a letter that states: "If you had been there, we would have doubtlessly reached a conclusion." There is no point in giving further examples. Sometimes there is the impression that God wishes to lead his own into situations where they cry to him: "Do you want us to work with you, yes or no? Are you with us, yes or no? Do you want us to drop you for easier masters and especially for those more grateful for what we do for you, yes or no?" There is a silence from God which overwhelms.

I am beginning to understand better what spiritual literature calls "the nights." I have just reread the writings of Thérèse of Lisieux. She confides to Mother Marie de Gonzague this thought plaguing her: "You dream of the eternal possession of the Creator of all these marvels, you believe that one day you will walk out of this fog which surrounds you! Advance, advance; rejoice in death which will give you not what you hope for but a night still more profound, the night of nothingness." Without playing the mystic, I think that this is the great proof of faith as confidence. This confidence that the example of Abraham illustrates marvelously, leading the son of promise to death, while keeping to himself its tragic character. "You can do with me what you want, I who understand nothing, but I continue to place confidence in you, I trust in you." Our friend Yossel Rakover says the same thing.

At the risk of appearing outdated, I want to conclude by affirming the necessity of contemplation. I think that without it we are not able to grasp what is implied by this faith-confidence of which I have just spoken. Yossel Rakover, Thérèse of Lisieux are contemplatives. They discover in themselves, in tears and silence, a mysterious space which God's Spirit inhabits. There is inscribed the certitude of faithfulness. A stubborn certitude . . . It brings with it an immense liberty and peace. Even if it happens that the Church causes suffering, that "Church officials" are unjust and slow-witted. Father de Lubac knew this:

> It may be that many things about the Church in the human context disappoint us. It may be also that we are there deeply misunderstood, without it being our fault. It may be that in the midst of the Church we have to undergo persecution. Patience and loving silence will then be valued better than anything; we will no longer have to fear the judgment of those who do not see the heart. We will think that the Church will never better give Jesus Christ than on these occasions when it offers to us the opportunity to be shaped to his passion. The proof will be perhaps richer, if it does not come from the malice of some persons, but from a situation

which is able to appear inescapable; for it is no longer enough then to overcome the malice by a general pardon or by forgetting the person who caused it. However, let us be happy before "the Father who sees in secret" (*Méditation sur l'Église*, p. 184).

Postscript

I have had in hand a text of some thirty pages of the French theologian Jean-Marie Tillard: "Are We the Last Christians?" It was the text from a public lecture, the conclusion of a colloquium that took place on November 24 and 25, 1996, at the Dominican University of Ottawa. It was the occasion of the presentation of a volume dedicated to Tillard to mark his twenty-five years as a professor at the faculty of theology at this university. A moving and disturbing text, suggestive and emblematic. It begins with the history of the Jew, Yossel Rakover, who in the full barbarism of Nazism in the ghetto of Warsaw in 1943 cries to God and confesses his faith, despite the silence of the Eternal.

I knew Tillard: a theologian of international renown, an expert on the Second Vatican Council, a writer of merit, a passionate man of dialogue, as much with the Orthodox world as with the Anglican. Of imposing stature, elegant, with a deep look which betrayed a hint of sadness even when he made quite funny jokes. You could encounter him in ecumenical gatherings or assemblies and university proceedings the world over.

But why this text, almost a summary of his books, veiled in sadness, a flood of questions, a call to God that he not abandon humanity? I called Tillard to express to him my surprise, my delight over his deep faith, and to ask him to comment on such and such a page of his text. I hoped to meet with him in Geneva or in Paris or in London or in Fribourg or even in Rome . . . A thin voice said to me: "Come to Ottawa; I am no longer able to travel."

I was paralyzed and only said to him: "Father, I will come to Ottawa." He answered me: "I am very happy, but it is very cold." A glacial cold. I knew it. As low as thirty degrees below zero. But perhaps Tillard intended the word "cold" in another sense, symbolically. Cold because spring is still far off in the Church. Cold because the steps toward the union of Christians are very slow. I cannot otherwise understand the recourse to the life of Yossel Rakover and his almost blasphemous cry: "I believe in the God of Israel, even if he has done everything to destroy the faith which I have in him."

I would have wished that it were snowing when I traveled the long street, rue Laurier, and was passing over the famous Canal Rideau because the temperature would have thus risen a few degrees. Numerous people were skating on the canal and were having fun. I have traveled this street many times to go to the university where Tillard awaited me. He received me in his room, full of all kinds of books. I was able to see large volumes of theology, patristics, history, but also literature, for Tillard was extremely well read. He speaks and writes an enthralling French. In 1977 he was made a Chevalier of the Legion of Honor for his contribution to the prestige of French culture. He loved to quote French authors; writers such as Fénelon, Pascal, Gide, Mauriac, Clavel . . . they fascinated him.

Tillard was born in 1927 on the island of Saint Pierre-et-Miquelon, French territory. An island tossed about by the winds of the Atlantic, partially harsh and rocky, partially covered with marshy ponds. Tillard returns to his homeland with memories of family and of the parish, the stories of customs, the symbolism of images. It is to a strange plant named "polygonum," that refuses to die even when it is totally uprooted, that he refers to reaffirm his faith in God who cannot leave lacerated and paralyzed human beings without hope. The "polygonum" rises again unexpectedly when it is least expected and becomes a bush that gives life and color to the island of the winds.

It is exactly like the Gospel of a certain Jesus of Nazareth, which the force of evil hounds in order to wipe out, along with his memory, his Church, his disciples who continue to cry as Rakover and as Tillard himself at the conclusion of his book: "I will always believe in you, even despite you."

The man who was before me spoke with a soft and mysterious voice of a man who continues to cry out his faith in the cold, the storm, the silence of the night. When he spoke to me, it was the history of the Church that I saw passing before my eyes: the early Church and the Church of today, the local church as a communion and the universal Church, the communion of Churches. He endlessly quoted Scripture as well as the tradition, made reference to the councils of all periods, mentioned phrases of the ancient Fathers and texts of theologians.

It was only after a few days that Tillard allowed himself to speak to me of his illness and his great desire to recover his health in order to take up again his work. Besides our long discussion, he had to prepare a text for the meeting of the Anglican-Catholic Commission in Toronto. A certainly important text, in view of the difficult relations between the two Churches, because of the ordination of women. Tillard truly loves Anglicanism. He has studied it thoroughly and keeps in close touch with the most important Anglican theologians. Already at the time of Cardinal Willebrands, who was president of the Secretariat for Christian Unity, Tillard had written and offered solutions to the thorny problem of the validity of Anglican ordinations.

He is no less interested in Orthodoxy. He knows its greatest theologians. The East continues to fascinate him because of its great closeness to the sources. It has models to offer on such questions as the exercise of the primacy of the Bishop of Rome and also matrimonial practice.

Tillard loves all historical periods; all are for him the time of God, even if God's presence is not always obvious nor his voice audible. He loves even these periods in the history of humanity or of the individual when God is not to be heard: the time of the silence of God and of the nights, tested and lived, not only by Jesus of Nazareth, but also by distant mystics like Teresa of Avila or Thérèse of Lisieux, as well as by recent witnesses such as Jacques Loew or Madeleine Delbrêl.

Tillard loves the Church that he compares to a small boat tossed by the winds, like the boats of his Atlantic island. And he dreams of the strength of the Spirit for the Church, rich in ancient experiences. For there is a sin, the worst of all: the sin against the Spirit that consists in being opposed to its renewing action. The glacial cold of the present is perhaps the voice of the Spirit who desires a Church more full of hope and capable of giving hope.

"Give us back reasons to hope!" Tillard said to me while telling me stories of people who ask it of the Church and Christians. There is the goal of Church: that it give itself to the future in mercy and faithfulness to its Savior.

Certainties (not countless), restlessness (sufficient), an enormous confidence in God, a very strong passion for ecumenism, a grounding in the history of the Christian faith, a heart full of tenderness for those who have lost their way: these are some of the qualities of one of the great people of our century before whom I have been moved.

I have admiration for his theology. For his person I can only report my emotion. Because he does not love to speak of himself, he does not neglect daily life; he constantly puts forward again the themes of communion and hope, reestablishes the reasons of faith in a language where rationality and poetry commune.

Thus I met Tillard in the glacial cold of the Canadian winter, in the expectation of spring when the "polygonum," mocking its detractors and those who try to root it out, becomes a shrub that continues to give life to the island beaten by storms.

Francesco Strazzari

Appendix

Some Dates

Jean-Marie Tillard was born in 1927 on the French island of Saint-Pierre-et-Miquelon (Canada). He joined the Dominican Order in the province of Saint-Dominique in Canada.

He received his doctor of philosophy degree from the University of Saint Thomas-d'Aquin in 1953; the license and readership (le lectorat) in theology at Saulchoir, in Paris, in 1957.

He was recognized "master in sacred theology" (a postdoctoral distinction within to the Order of Preachers) at the general chapter of Bogota in 1967.

He received the doctorate *honoris causa* from Trinity College in Toronto in 1978 and in 1980 from the University of Saint-Michel.

For theological research on Anglicanism, he received in 1981 the decoration of the Order of Saint Augustine of Canterbury.

In 1997 he was made Chevalier of the Legion of Honor for his contribution to the prestige of French culture.

Jean-Marie Tillard died on November 13, 2000.

Academic Positions

1957–60: Professor in the faculty of theology of the Dominican College of Philosophy and Theology in Ottawa.

1957–64: Visiting professor at the faculty of theology of the University of Laval in Quebec.

1957–65: Visiting professor at the Department of the Science of Religion of the University of Ottawa.

1960: Tenured professor at the faculty of theology of the Dominican College of Ottawa.

1966–80: Visiting professor at the International Center Lumen Vitae at Brussels.

1967–68: Visiting professor at St. John's College in Nottingham, England.

1969: Visiting professor at Oxford, St. Stephen's House, England.

1969: Visiting professor at Lincoln College in Lincoln, England

1975–81: Master of Studies at the Dominican College.

1981: Visiting professor at the University of Fribourg, Switzerland

1998: Visiting professor at the Ecumenical Orthodox Institute of Chambésy-Geneva, Switzerland.

Research and Consultations

1962–67: Expert and theological adviser to the Canadian episcopate at the Second Vatican Council (conciliar *peritus*).

1965–68: President of the Canadian Theological Society.

1969: Member of the Anglican-Roman Catholic International Commission.

1969: Member of the National Commission for the Union of Catholic and Anglican Churches, at Ottawa.

1969: Consultant for the Secretariat for the Unity of Christians, Rome.

1974–80: Member of the International Theological Commission, Rome.

1977: Member of the International Commission for the Dialogue with the Disciples of Christ, Rome-Indianapolis.

1977: Vice Moderator of the Commission on Faith and Order, of the World Council of Churches, Geneva.

1979: Member of the International Dialogue Commission between the Orthodox Church and the Roman Catholic Church.

1980: Member of the Paul VI Institute for research on Vatican II

1981–85: Member of the Board of the Ecumenical Institute at Tantur (Jerusalem).

1986: Member of the International Association Jacques-Maritain, Paris-Ottawa.

Research and Publications

Tillard was a specialist in dogmatic theology, especially ecclesiology. Since 1975 he centered his research on ecumenism. He was a world-recognized expert in this area. He was the author of many significant works.

He was the author of some thirty contributions in collective works and more than two hundred published articles in Canadian, American, and European journals.